Fast Breaks, Finger Rolls, and Fisticuffs: Memories of Big East Basketball

Mark Hostutler

Published by Service of Change, LLC

© 2016 by Mark Hostutler

ISBN: 978-0-6926691-3-6

www.ServiceOfChange.com

For Allison, my one and only.

Thank you for everything.

"A thing of beauty is a joy forever:
Its loveliness increases;
It will never pass into nothingness."

—John Keats, 1795-1821

Introduction

DESPITE MY RELATIVE YOUTH—I was born in 1980, not long before Mt. St. Helens erupted and John Lennon was assassinated—there are few things I can remember with clarity about my childhood, and fewer that don't involve sports. I'm not sure if it's the distance of age or the passage of time, but I have trouble recalling what I did last weekend without more concentration than should be required. My memories of adolescence are often hazy and out of focus, like pictures taken with no flash.

On a recent visit to my parents' house, with my wife and kids in tow, my mother asked me to sort through some of my stuff that had accumulated in our basement storage over the years. Since I had long ago moved out, and my parents' space was finally their own, she wanted me to figure out what could and could not be thrown out. Whatever was down there was either going with me or being tossed to the curb.

I came across some things I expected—piles of baseball cards and a mammoth collection of college basketball magazines from *Sporting News* and *Street & Smith's*—and more things I had not, like a towering stack of baseball helmets that once served as bowls for Dairy Queen ice cream. Collecting dust in the corner was a Nintendo console, prompting me to try to tally the unhealthy amount of time I spent controlling the video-game version of Bo Jackson in *Tecmo Bowl*.

I also unearthed shoeboxes full of VHS tapes, most of which contained the pay-per-view wrestling events—Royal Rumble, WrestleMania, SummerSlam, and Survivor Series—that, in my mind, once marked the seasons of the year. There was one giant moving box brimming with more than 30 tapes, however, that was dangerously close to our hot-water heater.

I read the meticulously crafted labels, and immediately recognized my handwriting from more than 20 years ago and the great lengths I took to avoid making a mistake. The tapes featured the entire 1993 and 1994 NCAA Tournaments.

That's correct: I recorded every second of those Big Dances. And if you think I recorded and never re-watched them, you're wrong. I watched Santa Clara and

1

freshman Steve Nash upset Arizona as many times as I watched Chris Webber travel, then call a timeout his team didn't have. That is to say I saw it dozens of times—that's how much I loved college basketball.

If only we could be as passionate about the things in our adult lives as we were about our hobbies as kids.

As I held those VHS tapes and thumbed through the dog-eared, yellowing pages of the season previews, I was not only reminded of my love for college hoops—which remains to this day, despite the myriad factors testing its strength—but particularly my interest in the Big East. It was a time when the game's stars who were ticketed for NBA glory stayed in college for at least three years, if not all four, allowing fans to develop a bond with them.

Back then, names like Billy Owens and Donyell Marshall meant more to me than George Bush and Bill Clinton, because the former pair presided over the landscape I cared most about. The Berlin Wall was demolished, the Soviet Union collapsed, riots destroyed Los Angeles, and the FBI raided a cult compound in Waco, Texas. Yet, I was pretty much oblivious to it all. I could, however, tell you who was leading the Big East in scoring, rebounding, assists, or blocks on any given night.

Even the coaches had me glued to the screen of my tube television, as I wondered what they would do or say next. Each one had a trademark—whether it was Lou Carnesecca's sweaters, John Thompson's towel, Jim Boeheim's thick-rimmed glasses, P.J. Carlesimo's lumberjack beard, or Rollie Massimino's theatrics—that made him seem like a cartoon character.

Yes, ESPN's Big Monday meant more to me than Taco Tuesday or Thirsty Thursday ever did.

I still mourn the conference's death, and the events that preceded it. With all due respect to the current iteration of the Big East, the real one was laid to rest years ago. The Big East lives on in name and spirit, but certainly not the flesh.

As someone with as much of an affinity for history as sports, you can imagine how many times I've been accused of mythologizing the past. I admit my tendencies to wax nostalgic on historical events make me sound like I'm from a generation that stored its money under the mattress. However, I'm not alone with my feelings for the Big East, as its beauty has given me and so many others a joy that will last forever.

"The advent of the Big East was one of the most important events in college basketball history," Carnesecca recently told me. "It exploded onto the scene. With all the coverage, the traditions, the players, and the charismatic coaches, you had such a beautiful picture."

Hindsight has enabled us to see that the Big East was born at the intersection of Blessing and Curse. In 1979, Providence athletic director Dave Gavitt

2

orchestrated the formation of the basketball-only alliance that included his Friars, Syracuse, Georgetown, St. John's, Seton Hall, Boston College, and Connecticut. (Villanova joined a year later, and Pittsburgh two years after that.) Gavitt gifted the world a conference that was like no other. In just its third year of existence, it produced the national runner-up. In its fifth year, it had the champion, and in its sixth year, three Final Four teams.

However, the Big East's disregard for football, cemented at its birth, and its inability to fully embrace the sport ultimately proved to be its undoing. (Although the conference began sponsoring football in 1991, when it added Miami into the mix, it created an unusual structure to the league. Tension quickly arose between the football and non-football schools, and the rest is history.) For all of the great moments that the mega-conference of the late 2000s and early 2010s gave us, like Syracuse's six-overtime victory over Connecticut and the Huskies' leap from ninth place in the league to first place in America, the 16-school setup was doomed to fail.

"The Big East paid the price," William C. Rhoden wrote in the *New York Times*, "for ignoring the implications of not having big-time football in its portfolio."

Football may be king in this country, but it isn't king in my heart. If you would've told the teenaged me that one day Syracuse would flee the Big East for a piece of the money pie generated by football, Kleenex would've run out of tissues. (I never imagined that Big East basketball would be added to the burgeoning body bag attributed to football.)

"The Big East was the greatest basketball alignment in the history of college basketball," said Rick Pitino. "Football is running our country right now. It is running rampant."

"I just hate where college athletics is going," said Larry Brown. "To see the Big East break up is real troubling."

Rhoden stated that "no conference has played better basketball than the Big East; other conferences have played college basketball longer, but none better."

Objectively speaking, I think the ACC might have a thing or two to say about that. But it's a moot point, because the modern configuration of the Big East is a mid-major compared to its former self.

The Big East Tournament, held at Madison Square Garden in midtown Manhattan, was once the perfect precursor to March Madness. And no one summed up its greatness better than *Yahoo! Sports* columnist Dan Wetzel:

"The Big East Tournament is the feeling that players get when they step onto the floor, especially in those electric weekend night sessions, just a block and a half off Broadway, when maybe Bill Clinton or Spike Lee or Denzel Washington arrives courtside.

"The Big East Tournament is a row of Wall Street guys sneaking away for an afternoon session, dressed in $1,000 suits as they slam drinks and berate some official that dared to make the wrong call on the Hoyas.

"The Big East Tournament is the throngs of twenty-something alums who have moved to the city, live in the neighborhood, and rush across 31st Street between sessions to the Blarney Stone or the Irish Times or Jimmy's BBQ for drinks and food, taking the opportunity to act up with their college buddies again or maybe to run into that girl they should've asked out back in the day.

"The Big East Tournament is the vast assortment of former players, playground legends, AAU coaches, agents, runners for agents, NBA executives, sneaker reps, high school coaches, hangers-on, and Brooklyn accents that fill the seats. This is the grassroots scene the NCAA would prefer you didn't notice, but everyone in the game recognizes as the engine of the sport."

Now, the Big East Tournament is just like all the others in the crowded lineup, no different than the Atlantic 10 or Mountain West. No offense to Xavier, Butler, Marquette, DePaul, and Creighton, but if your school is located more than 600 miles from the Atlantic Ocean, geography alone should prevent you from being a conference member. Indeed, the Big East is neither big, nor east anymore.

Mike Tranghese, who assumed Gavitt's helm as commissioner in 1990 and retired in 2009, said: "I have no forgiveness in my heart for how certain people [schools] left. I'll go to my grave with that."

Me, too. Like a middle-aged man suffering from a midlife crisis and searching for his fountain of youth, I decided to track down some of the guys who lived my dream of playing in the Big East. If I wanted to relive, if not memorialize the idyllic days of the conference, who better to turn to than the men who made the magic? The following players were happy to have me along as a passenger on their trip down memory lane. Many of them offered genuine thanks for being given a platform to share their thoughts and experiences about what they truly believed was a phenomenon like no other.

On Dec. 11, 1979, John Bagley scored 14 points to help Boston College defeat host Seton Hall, 82-61, in the first Big East basketball game. Exactly one month later, I was born.

The world has never been the same.

4

The Players

ABDUL ABDULLAH, PROVIDENCE, 1992-94

The 5-11 point guard was a teammate of current Friars coach Ed Cooley at Central High School in Providence. Abdullah went to two junior colleges before enrolling at Providence, where he was the perfect facilitator for a team with a handful of NBA talent. As a senior, his 8.0 assists per game were instrumental in the team's late-season run to the Big East Tournament title. Abdullah played briefly in Poland, and for the past 12 years, he has been a broker of both commercial and residential mortgages. He did a two-year stint as an assistant at Brown, and currently works part time as a business manager for Edge Sports International, an agency that represents and markets pro athletes worldwide.

DANYA ABRAMS, BOSTON COLLEGE, 1993-97

A native of New York's Westchester County, Abrams attended the Hackley School, an elite prep school in the village of Tarrytown, the setting of "The Legend of Sleepy Hollow." As a 6-7 senior, he was named the state's Mr. Basketball, a rare honor for a player outside the city. A 250-pound tight end and defensive end on the gridiron, Abrams received football offers from Notre Dame and Penn State, but he loved basketball and opted to play for B.C. A first-team All-Big East selection for three years, Abrams registered more than 2,000 points and 1,000 rebounds for the Eagles, and played 12 years overseas, mostly in Spain. (Consequently, he knew before anyone in the States  how much the Spaniards were sleeping giants on the international-hoops scene.) Now a resident of Avon, Mass., Abrams runs his own insurance practice.

RAFAEL ADDISON, SYRACUSE, 1982-86

The 6-7 small forward from Jersey City, N.J. ignored overtures from nearby Rutgers solely because it wasn't a member of the newly formed Big East. While with the Orangemen, Addison was routinely viewed by his coaches and teammates as one of the most underrated players in the country. As a junior in 1984-85, the conference's banner year, he was finally given his due by the media. Addison was named first-team All-Big East, along with Patrick Ewing, Chris Mullin, Ed Pinckney, and Pearl Washington. A second-round pick of the Phoenix Suns, he competed for six seasons in the NBA. Now back in Jersey City, Addison is a physical-education teacher on the elementary level, and his students generally have no idea that he played professional basketball.

RAFAEL ADDISON

MARQUES BRAGG, PROVIDENCE, 1988-92

The 6-8 power forward from East Orange, N.J. grew up with the members of the hip-hop group Naughty by Nature. A self-proclaimed late bloomer, Bragg played AAU ball alongside Eric Murdock, his future college teammate. Bragg's freshman season was Rick Barnes's first with the Friars, and although he wasn't one of the coach's recruits, he became one of his most important players. Bragg led Providence in rebounding as a junior and scoring as a senior, and played one season with the Minnesota Timberwolves. His services were in high demand in Europe, though, where he played the majority of his 13-year pro career. Bragg now owns his own construction company, and is an assistant coach at Division III New Jersey City University.

DONNY BROWN, PROVIDENCE, 1982-86

The 6-1 combo guard and product of South Central Los Angeles attended Verbum Dei, a basketball factory during his era. Being from the West Coast, Brown recalls having to prove himself to his teammates before his opponents. He did just that, although his Friars struggled during the majority of his time at Providence, particularly after Otis Thorpe's departure for the NBA. Brown led the team in scoring as a junior with just 9.5 points per game. Rick Pitino replaced Joe Mullaney as coach for Brown's senior year, and he appreciated the former's focus on individual development and conditioning, and was not surprised to see the Friars advance to the Final Four the year after he graduated. After living in Providence for 30 years, Brown recently moved back to Los Angeles, where he utilizes his experience in college recruiting to run a business that helps athletes get scholarships. His son, Matt Brown, graduated from Harvard, where he played both basketball and football.

FRED BROWN, GEORGETOWN, 1980-84

The 6-5 swingman from the Bronx and high school teammate of Ed Pinckney wanted to become a pilot, but his color blindness sabotaged his dreams of flying. As a freshman, Brown's norms—7.5 points, 3.9 rebounds, and 3.7 assists— garnered him the Big East Rookie of the Year award. A year later, his pass to an opponent in the waning seconds of the national championship sealed Georgetown's loss. Offseason knee surgery sidelined Brown for the majority of his junior year, and it sapped him of his explosiveness. To Brown's credit, he refused to let his career circle around the drain. He returned to the starting lineup as a senior, and led the Hoyas to their first crown. In 2007, Brown went public with his criticism of John Thompson, and what he believed was a lack of support for the players once they graduated. "I apologized to Coach Thompson for not communicating with him first, for not letting him know how I feel," said Brown. "But I'll stand by what I said five million years from now. Did I get any feedback for what I said? You bet. And a lot of it agreed with me." After a career as a financial advisor in the D.C. area, Brown is now retired and works for several nonprofits that give back to the community.

JOEY BROWN, GEORGETOWN, 1990-94

The 5-10 point guard was reared in the bayous of Louisiana, in Morgan City, a town of about 12,000 located 90 miles southwest of New Orleans. Brown was one in an unusually long pipeline of players from the Pelican State to attend

Georgetown. (Others included Steve Martin, Perry McDonald, Jaren Jackson, Johnathan Edwards, and Dwayne Bryant.) Brown credits his older cousin and high school teammate Dave Johnson (Syracuse) for drawing recruiters that far south, where they became intrigued by the point guard for his ability to set the tone defensively. As a high school sophomore, Brown developed his appetite for defense after being lit up for almost 50 points by Chris Jackson of Gulfport, Miss. At Georgetown, Brown started 123 of his 125 games, and as a junior, he averaged 10.7 points, 4.1 rebounds, and 6.2 assists. Now living in Houston, he is the vice president of his division at Travelers Insurance.

JOEY BROWN

SCOTT BURRELL, CONNECTICUT, 1989-93

SCOTT BURRELL

The Seattle Mariners drafted the multi-sport star from Hamden, Conn., who originally committed to Miami to play baseball, in the *first round*. However, a low offer from the Mariners, coupled with some tireless recruiting by Jim Calhoun and his assistant Dave Leitao, pushed Burrell toward college basketball. The years that followed have shown that the 6-7 small forward made the right choice. Burrell eventually played eight seasons in the NBA, including the 1997-98 campaign with the Chicago Bulls. He was a part of the team's eight-man playoff rotation and won a championship ring. Back living in his hometown, he is now the coach at Division II Southern Connecticut State.

9

BRYAN CAVER, SETON HALL, 1990-94

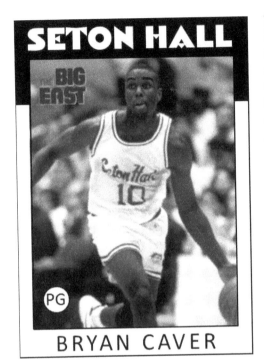

The 6-4 point guard from Trenton, N.J. engineered a pair of state championships as an upperclassman at McCorristin Catholic. Caver verballed to Syracuse, having visited the snowy campus with Jamal Mashburn. However, the players he competed against in high school—Terry Dehere and Jerry Walker—convinced him to compete with them in college. Caver averaged a workmanlike 12.0 points and 3.5 assists per game as a senior with the Pirates. He now works with special-needs children in Mercer County, N.J. and runs the basketball operations for Victory Sports, a group that aims to develop kids academically, socially, and physically.

ROBERT CHURCHWELL, GEORGETOWN, 1990-94

A product of Washington, D.C., the 6-6 wing remembers pretending to be Patrick Ewing when he was in middle school and often the tallest player on his team. In high school, Churchwell developed more hops than beer, capturing first place in the high, triple, and long jump at the conference championships in track and field. At Georgetown, he was often overshadowed by his highly touted teammates— Dikembe Mutombo, Alonzo Mourning, and Othella Harrington—a group he affectionately calls the "million-dollar crew." Officially, he played four games in the NBA, but hundreds more across the pond. Churchwell is now a Health and Physical Education teacher and high school coach in Richmond, Va.

BILL CURLEY, BOSTON COLLEGE, 1990-94

The 6-9 power forward grew up in soccer-crazed Duxbury, Mass., a coastal town and Boston suburb, and his New England accent remains thicker than clam

10

chowder. The McDonald's All-American led his high school to its first state championship in basketball, and committed to the Eagles, despite their 17-63 Big East record in the previous five seasons. Curley was named Big East Rookie of the Year as a freshman, and capped his illustrious career on The Hill by leading Boston College to one of the greatest upsets in NCAA Tournament history, a second-round victory over North Carolina. (The top-ranked defending champion featured Eric Montross, Jerry Stackhouse, Rasheed Wallace, Jeff McInnis, Derrick Phelps, and Kevin Salvadori, all of whom competed in the NBA.) The win landed Curley on the cover of *Sports Illustrated*, and not long after,

BOSTON COLLEGE

BILL CURLEY

he was selected in the draft's first round by the San Antonio Spurs. A variety of injuries derailed his professional career. Now back in Duxbury, Curley is the coach at Division III Emerson College.

TERRY DEHERE, SETON HALL, 1989-93

SETON HALL

TERRY DEHERE

The 6-2 shooting guard from Jersey City, N.J. was a machine programmed to score … and talk smack. As a senior, SHU's all-time leading scorer (2,494 points) earned Big East Player of the Year honors. Drafted 13th by the Los Angeles Clippers, Dehere will never forget the franchise's Christmas party his rookie year in the NBA. The party was held at a Beverly Hills building owned by then-Clippers owner Donald Sterling. Instead of being given silverware befitting the fancy occasion, attendees used plastic utensils to eat. And in 2014—when Sterling's stingy business practices came to light after his racist remarks got him banned from the league—the rest of the world knew why. Following a six-year career in

11

the NBA, Dehere returned to Jersey City, where he is now an affordable-housing developer and restaurateur.

ERIC EBERZ, VILLANOVA, 1992-96

The 6-7 native of western New York was named the *Buffalo News* Player of the Year as a senior in high school, four years after Duke's Christian Laettner won the award. The Eric Eberz that the college-basketball world came to know—a sharpshooter with uncanny range—was hardly that as a teenager. In his last two years of high school, he *attempted* a combined 41 3-pointers. (His height forced him to play under the rim.) As a junior at Villanova, he canned 94 triples. For all of the success he and his Wildcats had, he is often reminded by Philadelphia sports fans about the one game he'd like to forget: Villanova's triple-overtime loss to Old Dominion in the first round

ERIC EBERZ

of the 1995 NCAA Tournament. Eberz competed for seven years overseas, mostly in South Korea, dangerously close to the 38th Parallel, where he insists he was not the tallest player on his teams. Now, he and his wife's family manage a chain of pubs on Philadelphia's Main Line, including the one a mile from campus that is a popular watering hole for Villanova coaches.

STEVEN EDWARDS, MIAMI, 1992-96

STEVEN EDWARDS

The 6-6 wing and Miami native was a two-time Mr. Basketball in the state of Florida, and although he had offers from other more-established programs, he pledged his services to the hometown Hurricanes. His older brother, Doug Edwards, played at Florida State, while his younger brother, Allen Edwards, won two national championships at Kentucky. Steven led Miami—which didn't end a 14-year hiatus from the sport until as recently as 1985—in scoring for three seasons, as the basketball neophytes continued their uphill climb toward respectability in the Big East. A 12-year veteran of overseas basketball, he is back home in South Florida and works in credit-card processing.

PHIL GAMBLE, CONNECTICUT, 1985-89

The 6-4 shooting guard grew up as the youngest of nine children, all born to the same parents, in the projects of Washington, D.C. His father eventually abandoned the family, and Gamble was left to fend for himself. (All eight of his siblings spent time in prison.) The unprecedented success that the Huskies have recently experienced—four national championships in the last 18 years—can be traced back to the NIT crown that Gamble and his teammates won at the conclusion of the 1987-88 season, Jim Calhoun's second in command. To illustrate the rigors of the Big East at that time, Connecticut finished dead last in the conference with a 4-12 record, but went on to capture

the NIT title with five consecutive postseason victories. (Connecticut's conference record in the first nine years of the Big East was 44-86.) Gamble scored 14.7 points per game as a junior that year, and struck for a season-high 25 in the final against Ohio State to win MVP honors. He played briefly in Sweden and South Korea, now lives in Simsbury, Conn., and is toying with the idea of writing an autobiography. Considering the obstacles he has overcome—he survived skin cancer, as well as an apartment fire that destroyed all of the memorabilia from his career and forced him to escape from a broken window on the building's fourth floor—a book about his life would be one heck of a read.

BILLY GOODWIN, ST. JOHN'S, 1980-83

Born in Harlem and raised in the Bronx, the 6-5 shooting guard went to college in Queens after spending a season at San Jacinto in Texas. As a junior, Goodwin averaged career highs in points (14.7) and rebounds (5.5) for the Redmen. While toiling as a professional in the Continental Basketball Association, waiting for a call from the NBA, he decided to drop his dream of playing in the league, and sign

ST. JOHN'S

BILLY GOODWIN

a more lucrative contract overseas. "I remember seeing guys in the summer who played overseas, and they'd be driving Jaguars," Goodwin said. "I was making $500 a week in the CBA, and these other dudes were making $300,000 a month in Europe. So I went over there while my name was still fresh." He began playing in France in 1987, and he hasn't left the country since. Goodwin currently lives in Dijon, a city famous for its mustard, where he is fulfilling his dream of helping underprivileged kids. "If a child is born into a poor family, it's not their fault," he said. "They deserve to have fun like everyone else. That's why I've dedicated my life to helping put a smile on their faces."

MICHAEL GRAHAM, GEORGETOWN, 1983-84

Although the 6-9 power forward from Washington, D.C. played just one season for the Hoyas, no other player in Big East history personified the conference's rugged play like him. As a freshman, Graham appeared in 35 of Georgetown's 37 games, starting 17 of them, and averaged a mere 4.7 points and 4.0 boards per outing. But it wasn't his statistics that put him in the limelight. It was the protection he provided Patrick Ewing under the basket. Graham shaved his head well before it was fashionable, and his fiery presence gave the Hoyas what they lacked. Although he was portrayed as a malicious player by the media, he never fouled out of a game. The press built up the national championship against Houston to be a matchup between Ewing and Akeem Olajuwon. However, it was Graham who drew the task of defending the soon-to-be-nicknamed Dream. Graham contributed 14 points and five rebounds in the victory, and later appeared on the cover of *Sports Illustrated*, dunking over two Houston defenders. Academic issues prevented Graham from ever suiting up at Georgetown again. He bounced around the CBA, playing for coaches Phil Jackson, Cazzie Russell, and Henry Bibby. Now living in Waldorf, Md., Graham won a Powerball for $1 million in 2013.

OTIS HILL, SYRACUSE, 1993-97

The 6-8 center from White Plains, N.Y. shared a room with another blue chip from the Empire State at the Nike/ABCD camp in Oregon the summer before their senior year of high school. John Wallace convinced his roommate to sign with the Orangemen, although it didn't take much effort. Hill had already fallen in love with Syracuse as a child, watching Sherman Douglas toss alley-oops to Derrick Coleman and Billy Owens. Hill redshirted his first year on campus, then united with the versatile Wallace, as his muscle supplied the yin to Wallace's all-around yang in the frontcourt. Lacking the height coveted by NBA scouts, Hill made a living overseas for 12 years. Now back in New York, he works as a sort of corrections officer for juveniles who have committed serious crimes.

MALCOLM HUCKABY, BOSTON COLLEGE, 1990-94

The 6-2 guard and native of Bristol, Conn. could see ESPN's headquarters from the front porch of his childhood home. The Houston Astros drafted the two-sport star coming out of high school, but he was more interested in Big East basketball than professional baseball. As a scholastic senior, Huckaby carried Bristol Central to a perfect season that culminated with a state crown. The quartet of Huckaby, Bill Curley, Howard Eisley, and Gerrod Abram may not have been the most-ballyhooed class of recruits the Eagles have ever landed, but none accomplished more. Huckaby cracked the starting lineup as a sophomore, and averaged double figures in scoring for three straight seasons. Still living in New England, Huckaby is a financial advisor with Capitol Securities Management and a college basketball analyst for ESPN, announcing two games each week during the season.

JAREN JACKSON, GEORGETOWN, 1985-89

JAREN JACKSON

The 6-4 shooting guard and high school valedictorian from New Orleans honed his skills at Shakespeare Park, and recalls how Georgetown assistant coach Craig Esherick was a regular in the Big Easy in the mid-1980s. Jackson learned the ropes from David Wingate and Reggie Williams, and didn't become a full-time starter for the Hoyas until his senior season. That year, when Jackson averaged 12.3 points and 5.2 rebounds per game, the Hoyas barely avoided the dubious distinction of being the first No. 1 seed to ever lose in the first round of the NCAA Tournament. (No. 16 Princeton took Georgetown down to the wire before falling, 50-49.) Although he went undrafted, Jackson played in parts of 12 seasons in the NBA, including the strike-shortened 1998-99, when he won a championship with the Spurs. He has since been a head coach in the National Basketball League of Canada, as well as an assistant in the Development League. Now living in Indianapolis, he does commentary for the Fort Wayne Mad Ants when they play at home.

EARL KELLEY, CONNECTICUT, 1982-86

The 6-1 combo guard from New Haven, Conn. was a product of Wilbur Cross High School, a basketball powerhouse. As a junior, Kelley and the Governors dealt Patrick Ewing (Rindge and Latin from Cambridge, Mass.) the only loss of his scholastic career. A year later, Kelley led the nation in scoring, averaging 39.4 points before the dawn of the 3-point line. He scored 60 in one game, and 54 in another against Camden (N.J.), which featured Milt Wagner and Billy Thompson, a duo who'd later win a national championship at Louisville. One of 10 kids in his family, Kelley stayed home for college, and was named Big East Rookie of the Year as a freshman. He led the Huskies in scoring all four years. A fifth-round pick of the Spurs, Kelly never made it to the NBA, although he played overseas. He's now living back in New Haven, where he trains and mentors young players.

KERRY KITTLES, VILLANOVA, 1992-96

The 6-5 shooting guard from New Orleans led St. Augustine High School—a football factory that counts Tyrann Mathieu and Leonard Fournette among its alumni—to a state championship his senior year. Kittles was enamored of the Big East/ACC Challenge as a teenager, and chose Villanova because it met all the criteria he was looking for in a college. "It was small, outside a major city but not in the boonies, and Catholic, which was a big part of my upbringing," he said. Kittles humbly admits that, while he often excelled as a youngster in pickup against the players at Tulane and the University of New Orleans, he had no idea how good he would be on the next level. It didn't take long for him and the rest of the nation to find out. The Big East Player of the Year as a junior, Kittles finished as the Wildcats' all-time leading scorer (2,243 points) and remains atop the chart to this day. He was drafted eighth overall by the New Jersey Nets in a class that included Big East brethren Allen Iverson and Ray Allen, as well as Kobe Bryant, Stephon Marbury,

KERRY KITTLES

and Steve Nash. Kittles averaged a career-high 17.2 points per game in his second season with the Nets, and later started in the NBA Finals in back-to-back years. He currently lives in North Jersey.

JEROME LANE, PITTSBURGH, 1985-88

JEROME LANE

The 6-6 power forward's glass-shattering dunk—and ESPN analyst Bill Raftery's exclamation ("Send it in, Jerome!")—is one of the most iconic moments in college basketball history. Lane, a native of Akron, Ohio, attended Saint Vincent-Saint Mary, a high school made world famous almost 20 years later by another one of its ballers. At Pitt, despite yielding several inches to his competition in the post, he led the country in rebounding as a junior with 13.5 per contest. A first-round pick of the Denver Nuggets, Lane played in parts of five seasons in the NBA. Now back in Akron, he works for the city's customer-service department.

17

JASON LAWSON, VILLANOVA, 1993-97

The 6-10 center averaged 24.7 points, 14.9 rebounds, and 8.2 blocks per game as a high school senior in Philadelphia, yet he was considered to be the consolation prize that year for recruiters who wanted the best big man in the city. (Lawson's childhood friend, Rasheed Wallace, was the top-ranked blue chip in the nation's Class of 1993.) Rollie Massimino had pursued Lawson, but when the coach left for UNLV, Lawson was intent on signing with Virginia. Just a few hours before he was scheduled to put his name on the dotted line, new Wildcats coach Steve Lappas called Lawson, promising him a starting spot as a freshman. Four years later, Lawson had started 131 games and was

named the Big East's Defensive Player of the Year as a senior. As it does with Eberz, the scar tissue from Villanova's tournament loss to Old Dominion remains with Lawson. The second-round pick played in only 17 NBA games, and stuffed his bank account with money earned in Spain, France, and Greece, as well as Mexico and Jordan. Now back in Philadelphia, Lawson is a high school basketball coach in the city.

JOHN LINEHAN, PROVIDENCE, 1997-2002

Considering his penchant for thievery, one might say the 5-8 floor general played the game with criminal intent. Linehan developed his appetite for pressure defense in Chester, Pa., a hoops-loving city located between Philadelphia and Wilmington that also nurtured Jameer Nelson, Tyreke Evans, and Rondae Hollis-Jefferson. His scholastic battles with Lower Merion's Kobe Bryant, who stands almost a foot taller than Linehan, were epic. The Black Mamba paid tribute to Linehan well into his Hall of Fame career by telling reporters the toughest defender he'd ever faced was the Providence point guard. Linehan only had offers from Howard and

Coppin State coming out of high school, so he prepped for a year at The Winchendon School in Massachusetts, before signing with the Friars. Five seasons later—he missed the majority of 1999-2000 as a medical redshirt—all he did was supplant former Friar Eric Murdock as Division I's all-time steals leader. His 385 are still the record. As a senior, Linehan averaged 12.5 points, 3.8 boards, 4.4 assists, and *4.5 steals* per outing. He's now an assistant coach at Drexel.

FELIPE LOPEZ, ST. JOHN'S, 1994-98

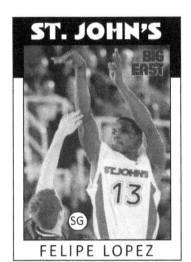

The 6-5 shooting guard and his family emigrated from the Dominican Republic when he was 14. Not long after landing in the South Bronx, Lopez began being hailed with the kind of hype that only the New York City media could generate and that few athletes could ever live up to. He committed to the Johnnies because of their "history," and appeared on the cover of *Sports Illustrated* before he even played a minute of college ball. Although the Red Storm never experienced the renaissance it was hoping for under him, he left Queens with almost 2,000 points in tow, and became a first-round pick of the Spurs. Lopez played four years in the NBA, and now does charity work with children.

BOBBY MARTIN, PITTSBURGH, 1987-91

The razor-thin, 6-9 forward and McDonald's All-American from Atlantic City, N.J. reneged on his oral commitment to Villanova, thus intensifying the bad blood between the programs that started with the courtship of Doug West. To this day, Martin won't forgive himself or his Panther teammates for losing to Ball State in the first round of the 1989 NCAA Tournament. As a junior, he averaged career highs in points (15.0) and rebounds (8.6). Martin's tenure as a professional overseas spanned 16 years, and during each offseason, he lived in Boston with his trainer, whom he credits for prolonging his career. Martin settled in the

19

area after his retirement, and now runs BMB Training and Development, paying it forward to the next generation of players.

JASON MATTHEWS, PITTSBURGH, 1987-91

The 6-3 wing was reared in the urban core of Los Angeles, competing with and against the likes of Chris Mills, Sean Higgins, Trevor Wilson, and Brian Williams (the late Bison Dele). As a preteen, he was more interested in baseball and football, until his best friend Josh Oppenheimer (now an assistant coach of the Milwaukee Bucks) convinced him to ditch the sports in favor of basketball. Matthews was a UCLA ball boy and fell in love with the game in 1984, when Pauley Pavilion hosted the West Regionals of the NCAA Tournament, and he worked Patrick Ewing and Georgetown's Sweet 16 win over UNLV. He and Oppenheimer used to rebound for (former Bruin) Reggie Miller during his individual  shooting sessions, when he would hoist 1,500 jumpers and 500 free throws per day. Still living in Pittsburgh, Matthews is now a successful businessman, having founded W. Blazer Holdings, a company named in honor of his AAU team, the Westside Blazers, that caters to clients in the energy and real-estate markets.

DWAYNE MCCLAIN, VILLANOVA, 1981-85

As a high school senior, the 6-6 shooting guard from Worcester, Mass. and his Holy Name teammates may have lost to Patrick Ewing's Rindge and Latin in the Massachusetts state final in the Boston Garden. However, it was McClain who, as a college senior, got the last laugh, as his David slew Ewing's Goliath. He painted his Mona Lisa in the national championship, scoring a game-high 17 points to nudge the previously unranked Wildcats past heavily-favored Georgetown, to secure what has become known as perhaps the greatest upset in the history of team sports. In the more than 30 years since that victory, it has become the subject of a documentary and book. McClain, a second-round pick of the Indiana Pacers, played one season in the NBA and several more all over the globe. Now living in Jupiter, Fla., he is the co-founder and CEO of McClain's Mergers & Acquisitions, which provides assistance to businesses being sold or bought.

ANDRE MCCLOUD, SETON HALL, 1982-86

While he was doggedly pursuing the 6-6 forward's commitment, new Pirates coach P.J. Carlesimo sold McCloud on the opportunity to contribute immediately. The native of Washington, D.C. recorded astronomical numbers, as he led Seton Hall in scoring all four years and rebounding three. However, the Pirates struggled during his time on campus, and a number of his teammates transferred, amid rumors that Seton Hall might get kicked out of the conference. McCloud assured Carlesimo that he wasn't going anywhere, and that he wanted to help lay the foundation for the program's future. McCloud did just that as the freshman class when he was a senior eventually carried the Pirates to the

national-championship game. McCloud played professionally for 17 seasons in Europe, and now coaches football and basketball in Sarasota County, Fla.

ROGER MCCREADY, BOSTON COLLEGE, 1982-86

The 6-5 small forward from Brooklyn paired with Chris Mullin, a year McCready's elder, at Xaverian High School, to lead the team to a state championship in 1981. McCready had a reputation for playing bigger than his height would suggest, and his 18.1 points and 5.5 rebounds per game as a senior led the Eagles in both categories. He forsook a potential career overseas, saying "I didn't want to alienate myself in a foreign country for 10 months a year to prolong something that was not going to happen [playing in the NBA]." McCready became an assistant coach at Yale and Columbia, then earned his law degree from Hofstra. He is currently an Assistant District Attorney in Brooklyn.

JERRY MCCULLOUGH, PITTSBURGH, 1991-96

The 6-3 point guard and son of Harlem is one of a number of great players—a group that includes Felipe Lopez, Andre Barrett, and Kemba Walker—to have attended the now-defunct Rice High School. He joined his AAU teammates and fellow New Yorkers, Eric Mobley and Orlando Antigua, with the Panthers. As a sophomore, McCullough led Pitt in scoring and assists, when the team secured its lone tournament bid during his tenure. A torn ACL forced him to redshirt the 1994-95 season, but he regained his form the following year and again topped the Panthers in both statistical categories. McCullough is currently on Antigua's staff at South Florida, as the Director of Basketball Operations.

LANCE MILLER, VILLANOVA, 1989-93

The 6-6 small forward won three consecutive state championships at Bridgewater-Raritan West High School in New Jersey. His elder teammates—cousin Eric Murdock and brother David Miller—preceded him in the Division I ranks. The Wildcats had seen better days during Miller's tenure on the Main Line, when he led the team in scoring three years in a row. However, his exploits as a sophomore propelled Villanova to an unlikely NCAA Tournament berth. Miller's last-second free throws enabled the eighth-place Wildcats to win the play-in game of the Big East Tournament by a point. Then, an upset of top-seeded Syracuse earned them an at-large bid to the Big Dance with a 16-14 record. Miller currently lives in Somerset, N.J., working as a car salesman and coaching AAU ball.

DARREN MORNINGSTAR, PITTSBURGH, 1989-92

The 6-10 center from tiny Stevenson, Wash. averaged 32.2 points per game as a senior in high school against mostly inferior competition. Morningstar admittedly made a mistake by enrolling at Navy, but he quickly transferred to Pitt. As a senior with the Panthers, he averaged 12.3 points and 6.2 boards as a third-team All-Big East selection. A second-round draft pick, Morningstar played 23 games in the NBA and more in the CBA and overseas. Now a financial advisor in western Pennsylvania, he is the vice president of his own group at Morgan Stanley. His daughter, Meg Morningstar, plays volleyball at Notre Dame after being the Keystone State's Gatorade Player of the Year as a senior in high school.

MIKE MOSES, ST. JOHN'S, 1983-85

The 5-11 point guard led the now-defunct St. Nicholas of Tolentine in the Bronx—which later graduated Malik Sealy, Adrian Autry, and Brian Reese—to a state championship his senior year. Moses played at Florida with his AAU teammate Ronnie Williams, who remains the Gators' all-time leading scorer. After suffering through two losing seasons in Gainesville under coach Norm Sloan, Moses transferred back home. After sitting out a year, he immediately moved into the Redmen's starting lineup as a junior. Of course, a year later, St. John's put together a dream season, advancing to the Final Four with Moses as the floor general. He played one year in the United States Basketball League and one year in Germany, before becoming an assistant coach at Maine, Xavier, Delaware, and Rutgers. Now a school counselor, Moses lives in Walnut Creek, Calif.

LAWRENCE MOTEN, SYRACUSE, 1991-95

LAWRENCE MOTEN

The 6-5 shooting guard grew up in Washington, D.C., in Georgetown country, but never once entertained the idea of suiting up for the Hoyas, because their style of play conflicted with his. Instead, Moten followed his friend, future Canadian Football League quarterback Marvin Graves, to Syracuse, where he was named Big East Rookie of the Year as a freshman. All Moten did in central New York was become the Orangemen's all-time leading scorer, as well as the record-holder for the most points scored in conference play. No one in that region will ever forget his trademark, knee-high tube socks, the ones he claims made him look like "Superman

23

without a cape." Although he and Billy Owens were never teammates, their wives were roommates at Syracuse, and Owens is the godfather of Moten's children. A second-round pick of the Vancouver Grizzlies, Moten played three years in the league. Now living in Bowie, Md., he is an assistant coach at Division III Gallaudet University, a school for the Deaf located a block from his childhood home.

JAY MURPHY, BOSTON COLLEGE, 1980-84

The 6-9 power forward from Meriden, Conn. was a freshman at Chestnut Hill when news of the infamous point-shaving scandal broke. Murphy can vividly recall playing against Holy Cross, and its students taunting the Eagles by waving money and razor blades at them. Murphy was a key figure during the most successful four-year stretch in program history, as Boston College advanced to two Sweet 16s and an Elite Eight with him manning the frontcourt. His 19.8 points and 7.3 boards per outing as a senior merited him first-team All-Big East honors. A second-round pick, Murphy competed in 67 NBA games in four years with the Clippers and Washington Bullets. Now living in Wakefield, R.I., he is the Vice President of an Axia Insurance group. Murphy has three sons—Erik, Alex, and Tomas—who have dual citizenship in Finland, where their mother was born. Erik, who was drafted by the Bulls in 2013, and Alex often represent the country in international competition.

JOHN PINONE, VILLANOVA, 1979-83

The 6-8 center from Hartford, Conn. faced tremendous pressure to remain in-state and become a Husky. Connecticut's loss was Villanova's gain, as Pinone led the Wildcats in scoring all four of his seasons, which included four trips to the NCAA Tournament, with the latter two ending in the Elite Eight. He played in just seven games in the NBA for the Atlanta Hawks, before competing in Spain for a decade. Pinone currently works in commercial real estate and for the Archdiocese of Hartford, overseeing more than 30 cemeteries in the region. He has been a high school basketball coach for the last 18 years, and his team—Cromwell High School—won the small-school state title in 2009.

CONSTANTIN POPA, MIAMI, 1991-95

The 7-3 center with the trademark sky hook from Romania arrived in the United States barely speaking English. He finished high school at Virginia's Fork Union Military Academy, then joined the Hurricanes, whose coach, Leonard Hamilton, first showed interest in him when he was at Oklahoma State. Popa entered college

CONSTANTIN POPA

at a scrawny 195 pounds, was placed on a 10,000-calories-a-day diet, and eventually filled out to 225 pounds. His Miami teams were the punching bags of the Big East, until his senior year, when the Hurricanes finished .500 in the league and earned an NIT berth. A second-round draft pick of the Clippers, he nonetheless never played in the NBA, but competed overseas. Popa played long enough in Israel to obtain citizenship. Now, the married father of five has a wife who graduated from Syracuse and a daughter currently attending the school, but he doesn't hold it against them. He is the women's coach at Division II University of Indianapolis, where his Greyhounds are a fixture in the NCAA Tournament.

DARELLE PORTER, PITTSBURGH, 1987-91

The 6-4 combo guard and native of Pittsburgh grew up catching passes from future West Virginia quarterback Major Harris, while playing pickup football in the Steel City. Porter, an accomplished wide receiver, ultimately chose to play basketball in college, and he was one-fifth of the greatest recruiting coup in the history of Pitt hoops. It should come as no surprise that the coach responsible for securing the commitments of Porter, Jason Matthews, Sean Miller, Brian Shorter, and Bobby Martin was Panthers assistant John Calipari. Despite winning the Big East regular season as freshmen, they never got past the second round of the NCAA Tournament, and therefore drew a

DARELLE PORTER

measure of criticism. As a junior, Porter led the conference in assists with 7.9 per outing. After his playing days ended, he quickly ascended the coaching ladder, and became the skipper at Duquesne at age 28. He resigned from the post after three seasons, and now runs Ozanam, Inc., a nonprofit that helps Pittsburgh's youth develop academically, socially, and athletically.

DAVID RUSSELL, ST. JOHN'S, 1979-83

The unassuming, 6-7 swingman from Bellport on Long Island was the Big East's first Rookie of the Year, as he averaged double figures while shooting 62.4 percent from the field as a freshman. His scoring only increased thereafter, as he totaled more than 1,700 points for the Redmen. A second-round pick of the Nuggets, Russell never played in the NBA. However, his career overseas spanned 16 seasons, mostly in Spain. Russell is a member of the Suffolk (N.Y.) Sports Hall of Fame, along with fellow ballers Tom Gugliotta, Mitch Kupchak, and Jeff Ruland and baseball players Carl Yastrzemski and Craig Biggio. He is currently a mechanic for the Long Island Rail Road.

DAVID RUSSELL

SHAWNELLE SCOTT, ST. JOHN'S, 1990-94

SHAWNELLE SCOTT

The 6-10 center grew up in Harlem, living in a building that appeared in *New Jack City*, a movie about a housing project befallen by drug dealers. Like so many others before and after him, Scott used basketball to escape the dire straits of his childhood in the Big Apple, in a part of the city tourists try to avoid. At St. John's, he was a stabilizing force as the Redmen transitioned to the post-Carnesecca era. A second-round pick of the Portland Trail Blazers, Scott had a cup of tea in the NBA, before playing in Italy, Puerto Rico, China, and Greece. He is currently a teacher and coach at Millennium Brooklyn High School.

RONY SEIKALY, SYRACUSE, 1984-88

The 6-10 center was born in Beirut, Lebanon and grew up in Athens, Greece. However, there was little doubt in his mind that he would go to college in central New York. (His sister and an uncle attended Syracuse.) During his junior and senior seasons with the Orangemen, Seikaly paired with Derrick Coleman to form an imposing frontcourt. In the 1987 NCAA Tournament, his 33 points against Florida in the Sweet 16 and his 26 points and 11 rebounds against North Carolina in the Elite Eight powered Syracuse on its trek to the final. A lottery pick of the expansion Miami Heat, Seikaly won the NBA's Most Improved Player Award in the second of his 11 seasons in the league. In 1992-93, he averaged 17.1 points and 11.8 boards per

game for the Heat. Still living in South Florida, Seikaly works in real estate during the day and, after hours, is a prominent DJ on the nightclub scene.

DICKEY SIMPKINS, PROVIDENCE, 1990-94

The 6-9 center from the D.C. metro area was a part of the highest-rated recruiting class—along with Michael Smith, Troy Brown, and Rob Phelps—the Friars have ever landed. In his final year at Providence, the Friars won the Big East Tournament, and entered the NCAAs as one of the hottest teams in the country. However, they fell in the first round to Alabama and future NBA players Antonio McDyess and Jason Caffey. Simpkins was drafted late in the first round by the Bulls, with whom he won three championships as a reserve. He played parts of seven seasons in the NBA and several more in Europe. Now a scout for the Charlotte Hornets, Simpkins has been a television analyst at ESPN and

Fox since 2007, and is the founder of Next Level Performance, a company that sponsors AAU teams in the Chicago area and trains players of all skill levels.

CHRIS SMITH, CONNECTICUT, 1988-92

The 6-3 point guard and product of Bridgeport, Conn. may have had a name akin to John Doe's, but his game was anything but ordinary. As a kid, Smith and his friends used to record Syracuse games, then try to imitate the moves of Dwayne "Pearl" Washington out on the playground. Smith became good friends with Billy Owens from attending so many All-American camps together, and Owens tried hard to get Smith to join him with the Orangemen. However, despite the Huskies' struggles in the 1980s, Smith chose to stay close to home, so his family and friends could watch him play. In the quarter-century since he graduated, UConn has become one of the most prosperous programs in the country. But it was Smith and his comrades who first tasted tournament success. He eventually suited up for the Timberwolves for three seasons. Now a probation officer in the state of Connecticut, Smith remains the Huskies' all-time leading scorer.

CHRIS SMITH

JERRY WALKER, SETON HALL, 1989-93

The 6-7 bruiser was a product of one of the greatest high school programs in the country at St. Anthony in Jersey City, N.J. and was a key cog of arguably the best scholastic team ever. As a senior, his contributions, coupled with the overall brilliance of teammates Bobby Hurley and Terry Dehere, propelled the Friars to an undefeated season and No. 1 national ranking. Walker and Dehere took their talents up the road to East Rutherford, right after the Pirates had advanced to the NCAA Tournament final. During Walker's collegiate career, the Pirates

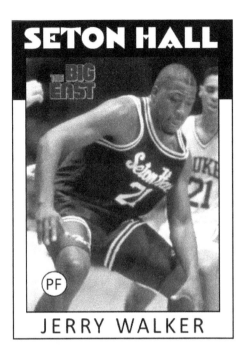

SETON HALL

JERRY WALKER

experienced a stretch of success—a pair of Big East Tournament titles and an Elite Eight berth—that hasn't been duplicated since. Although he was often overshadowed by Dehere and Arturas Karnishovas, Walker was a double-double waiting to happen, as evidenced by the 13.8 points and 7.4 rebounds he averaged as a junior. He played seven years abroad in Spain and Turkey. Back home in Jersey City, he is a community activist and the President and CEO of Team Walker, Inc., a nonprofit organization dedicated to helping the city's youth. Team Walker teaches kids life skills like preventing alcoholism and teen pregnancy while giving them an outlet to play sports.

JOHN WALLACE, SYRACUSE, 1992-96

The 6-8 power forward was reared in Rochester, N.Y. and thus indoctrinated in the Syracuse-Georgetown rivalry at an early age. No conference other than the Big East even existed in his mind, as four of his five official visits were to conference schools. A stat-sheet stuffer like few others in the nation, Wallace averaged 22.2 points and 8.7 rebounds per game as a senior and carried the fourth-seeded Orangemen to the NCAA Tournament final. He played seven years in the NBA and even earned an acting credit for his role in *He Got Game*. Wallace now works in public relations and fan development for the New York Knicks, and is very active in the world of charity.

SYRACUSE

JOHN WALLACE

ROBERT WERDANN, ST. JOHN'S, 1988-92

The 7-0 center and McDonald's All-American had the pleasure of playing with Kenny Anderson and the privilege of playing for Jack Curran at Archbishop Molloy High School in Queens. (The famed Curran won 972 of the 1,409 games he coached in 55 years at Molloy.) Mike Krzyzewski and Bobby Cremins were among the coaches who gave Werdann their sales pitch in his living room. But there was never any doubt about where Werdann was headed, as he started immediately for the Redmen, who liked to use his passing skills out of the high post. As a junior in the NCAA Tournament, he packaged 21 points, six boards, and four blocks to help St. John's oust top-seeded and Jimmy Jackson-led Ohio State in the Sweet 16. A torn calf sabotaged Werdann's senior year, but he was nonetheless drafted by the Nuggets in the second round. He played 47 games in the NBA, and had several stints in the CBA. Upon retirement, he began coaching, and has since been an assistant with three different franchises. Now living in Charlotte, he is a scout for the Detroit Pistons, and aims for a return to the bench.

DOUG WEST, VILLANOVA, 1985-89

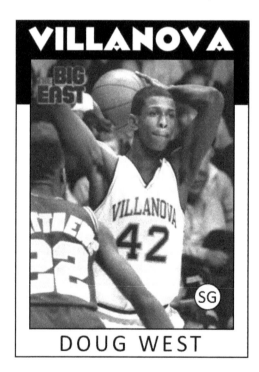

VILLANOVA

42

SG

DOUG WEST

The 6-7 shooting guard from Altoona, in central Pennsylvania, was the subject of a tug-of-war between Villanova and Pittsburgh, the Big East programs situated at opposite ends of the Keystone State. West signed with the Wildcats prior to their Cinderella run to the championship during his senior year of high school. After revealing that an oral surgeon and member of Pitt's board of trustees who lived in West's hometown offered him $10,000 to commit to the Panthers, things got ugly. The Pitt students welcomed West to the Fitzgerald Field House his freshman season in a manner that prompted his coach, Rollie Massimino, to say, "It's a farce, a disgrace. If that's the way it has to be, then I don't want to be a part of it, because people have to realize it's only a game." (Be sure to read further to hear West's comments.) The officials whistled the two teams for a combined 68 fouls that evening. West went on to play 12 years in the NBA, the first nine of which were with the expansion Timberwolves. During the 1992-93 season, he averaged 19.3 points per game, while shooting 51.7 percent from the floor. To put latter statistic in perspective, the similarly positioned Kobe Bryant has never shot better than 46.9 percent in a season. Now, West is back home as the coach at Division III Penn State Altoona.

JEROME WILLIAMS, GEORGETOWN, 1994-96

The 6-9 power forward, aptly nicknamed the Junkyard Dog, was the embodiment of a Hoya. He initially earned his toughness as a teenager in the nation's capital, playing pickup ball with Grant Hill, Exree Hipp, and Don Reid. Williams always wanted to play at Georgetown, but began to worry as the possibility of doing so became more of a reality. The school's academic reputation and the prospect of not qualifying caused him many sleepless nights. He spent two years at a nearby junior college, after which Georgetown welcomed him with open arms. He averaged a double-double in his first season with the Hoyas, who, with Allen Iverson and Othella Harrington, were loaded with talent. A late first-round pick of the Pistons, Williams found his niche as a workhorse in the NBA, playing nine years in the league. He now lives in Las Vegas and works as the founder of Champions Basketball Network, an online broadcasting company.

The Q & A

**WHAT WERE YOUR EARLIEST MEMORIES
OF BIG EAST BASKETBALL?**

DANYA ABRAMS, BOSTON COLLEGE: "When and where I grew up, you wanted to play in the Big East. You watched all the games on TV. It was the be-all, end-all. It didn't matter what school—you just wanted in. If you only got one scholarship offer, that's where you were going. Fortunately, I got a few."

RAFAEL ADDISON, SYRACUSE: "Growing up in the '70s, you watched mostly ACC games and Notre Dame. As an inner-city kid who's never been anywhere, I wanted to go to those places. But when the Big East formed, I said, 'Hold up. I can get away from home, but stay close enough at the same time.' I remember watching Syracuse in the [1981] NIT finals against Tulsa. The coach, the playing style, the uniforms—I said, 'Wow, that's me!' But when I got to upstate New York, I thought I was in another country. It might as well have been Italy!"

BILL CURLEY, BOSTON COLLEGE: "We always followed Patrick Ewing, because he was from Massachusetts, but my real association with the Big East didn't come until I was a freshman in high school. I'd watch the reruns of the Big Monday games in the afternoon when I got home from school. I used to love seeing Georgetown get in all those fights."

ERIC EBERZ, VILLANOVA: "I was a huge Syracuse fan growing up. Jim Boeheim was always at my games and in my house. I remember Keith Smart hitting that last-second jumper [to help Indiana beat Syracuse in 1987 for the national championship] and crying all night. Looking back, I'm not really sure why I didn't go to Syracuse. I verballed to Boston College and visited Florida State just so I could go to their football game against Miami. But I ended up choosing Villanova, and Boeheim still hasn't forgiven me."

JEROME LANE, PITTSBURGH: "I lived in Big Ten territory and was an Ohio State fan, but, man, the Big East had it going on!"

BOBBY MARTIN, PITTSBURGH: "My earliest memory was of Michael Graham absolutely scaring the shit out of everyone on the basketball court. That guy intimidated everyone. I also remember Willie Glass coming back home during the summers, wearing his Nike gear from St. John's. I thought it was sharp, and wanted to look like that."

JASON MATTHEWS, PITTSBURGH: "Living on the West Coast, we'd rush home after school to catch that first game on Big Monday. The hype of the Big East, the rivalries—that did it for me. My high school coach would do fundraisers so he could send a player to Five-Star [Camp at Robert Morris College, near Pittsburgh] every summer. I went before my senior year, and that's when [Pitt assistant] John Calipari started to recruit me. I wanted to go to Maryland, because [Terrapins coach] Lefty Driesell gave his guards the freedom to do whatever they wanted. But when Len Bias died [of a cocaine overdose], my mom put an end to that. So I was bound for the Big East."

JOHN PINONE, VILLANOVA: "My first year in college coincided with the first year of the Big East. We all had a chip on our shoulder, because we were out to prove that this was a legitimate league. The media would say that the Big East is good, but it's not as good as the ACC. I'm not sure what transpired early on that gave us the reputation of being a contact, physical league. It's probably that we were tougher kids. In the Big East, you couldn't back down. Opponents would smell fear. If you backed down, you were done. They'd try to kill you."

SHAWNELLE SCOTT, ST. JOHN'S: "I was 12, 13 years old when St. John's went to the Final Four. I was really impressionable, and Walter Berry and that left-handed white kid from Brooklyn [Chris Mullin] became my idols. So, when I was a high school senior, it came down to St. John's and Tennessee. I'll never forget what sealed my commitment. [St. John's assistant coach] Ron Rutledge was recruiting me, and they had just lost to Duke in the second round of the [1990 NCAA] Tournament. He called me and all he said was, 'Do you want to go to Tennessee and have cows watch you play? Or do you want to play in the Garden in front of thousands of people?' Then he hung up. And that was it."

TALK A LITTLE ABOUT YOUR RECRUITMENT AND
WHAT YOU REMEMBER MOST ABOUT THE PROCESS.

ABDUL ABDULLAH, PROVIDENCE: "I took a longer route to the Big East than most others. I'm originally from Brooklyn, and when I was nine years old, my father was shot and killed. He'd been separated from my mother for a while, and she had already remarried. I just remember needing money to buy some clothes for a school play, and my father said he'd drop off the money on a Tuesday, but he never did. By Thursday, my aunt told me that he'd passed away. I mean, how do you process that at that age? I was ashamed to cry at the funeral, and didn't approach his casket, because seeing his face rearranged like that was too much. He had a bad look on his face. My mother and step-father packed us up and moved us to Providence. It was a smaller city and a bit calmer than New York. By the time I got to high school, my mother and her husband moved to Morocco. There was no way I was going, so I stayed in Providence with an aunt. I lived off my father's social-security benefits, and went from being raised in a strict Muslim household, where I couldn't talk on the phone, to pretty much being on my own. As I got older, I started running with the wrong crowd, and my grades dropped. We had a basketball dynasty at my high school, but mentally, I was just floating around. I don't know how to describe it. After games, I'd see my teammates being embraced by their families, each guy walking off the court with his father's arm around him. Seeing that obviously affected me, but back then, I couldn't put into words how. I had to go to junior college at CCRI [Community College of Rhode Island], but I never finished my second year. [Arizona State coach] Bill Frieder was recruiting me really hard, and he got me set up at Compton Junior College, where I could earn enough credits to transfer. I lived with a friend in Inglewood, and took a bus to Compton every day. Meanwhile, Providence had just lost in the first round of the [1992] Big East Tournament, and were hurting for a true point guard. [Coach] Rick Barnes asked [*Providence Journal* sportswriter] Bill Reynolds, 'Where the hell is Abdullah? We need him.' Bill, who I'm close with to this day, called me out in California, and said, 'Hey, they want you.' I couldn't wait to get home. I was out there when the [Rodney King] riots happened. People were out there stealing stuff from stores like it was theirs. I found out Arizona State was recruiting another guard ahead of me, so I felt betrayed, and signed with Providence. I think I came in 30 pounds overweight."

DONNY BROWN, PROVIDENCE: "I had signed with San Francisco [as a senior in high school] in the spring of 1982, but a few months later in July, the school dropped the program. Quintin Dailey had been arrested for allegedly sexually assaulting a nursing student, and when he pled guilty to a lesser charge [of aggravated assault], he admitted to receiving money from boosters for no-show jobs. It was the culmination of a lot of prior infractions, so San Francisco self-imposed the death penalty, and gave all their players their release. School was going to start in a month, and I had nowhere to go. I visited Oklahoma State, UAB, and Providence all in a row. I didn't really know anything about Providence, but I chose it because of the conference. I was intrigued by the prospect of playing in the major arenas of these major cities."

FRED BROWN, GEORGETOWN: "I was not one to watch college basketball or pro basketball. I just played basketball. I couldn't tell you what a conference was. I didn't know who John Thompson was. [Georgetown assistant coach] Bill Stein approached me at a summer tournament, and said, 'The big fella is watching you.' I had no clue what he was talking about. Dean Smith came up to me once, and gave me his card. I didn't know who he was, either. I wanted to go to BYU; I loved all that open space in Utah. But my mother told me that wasn't happening. If I had my druthers, I'd have gone to Harvard, but my SATs weren't quite high enough. I chose Georgetown because D.C. seemed like a clean city with not as much crime, compared to New York. Plus, they had a black coach. I wanted a role model, someone who could identify with my struggles. I saw Georgetown play once at Madison Square Garden, and I like their tenacity and the way they played defense."

JOEY BROWN, GEORGETOWN: "I was a home body from a small town in Louisiana, and had never really been away. When I visited Georgetown and Washington, D.C., I was awestruck. Most people on their visits want to go out and party and have a good time. Not me. I was timid. So later, when I called Coach Thompson to tell him I was committing to Tulane, he said he was disappointed but not surprised. When Tulane faxed over the letter of intent, my high school coach never gave it to me. He hid it from me, wouldn't let me sign it. He just told me to think about it for a few hours. I'm glad he did. I came to realize that I couldn't let my fear of leaving home prevent me from a great opportunity like playing at Georgetown and in the Big East."

PHIL GAMBLE, CONNECTICUT: "My father used to beat on my mother, but when my brothers got old enough to stop him, he left the family. So my mother moved the family from North Carolina to D.C., where I grew up in the projects and would play ball on the courts outside our building until one, two o'clock in the morning. I remember playing one-on-one against Wayne Perry, the hitman, but I didn't know it until the next day, when my friends told me who he was. I went to St. Anthony [High School], where John Thompson used to coach back in the day. There was a whole section in the trophy case at the school from all the stuff his teams won. Coach Thompson heavily recruited me at Georgetown, and everyone figured I'd go there. But one time, when I thought he was coming for a home visit, my mother fixed the place up, and spent what little money she had on some food. You know, we were on public assistance, and she wanted our home to look nice. Coach pulled up outside my building, and called me from his car phone. He told me to come downstairs and get in the car, that we were going to see an academic advisor or something. I said, 'I thought you were coming in.' He said, 'Nah, I'll do that another time.' I told my mother and brothers that he wasn't coming in, and I could tell from the look on their faces that I wasn't going to Georgetown. Soon after, I committed to UConn, and the headline in the paper read, 'Gamble chooses UConn over Georgetown.' My mother was really disappointed Coach Thompson didn't come inside."

BILLY GOODWIN, ST. JOHN'S: "As a child, I went to all of Lou Carnesecca's camps. He never really seemed like he wanted me to go to St. John's. After my first year of junior college, he and his staff thought I'd be doing a second year. So when they found out I wasn't, and that I'd already visited UNLV, Texas A&M, and Oklahoma, they brought me and my parents in. Louie goes, 'Billy, what's this I hear you're visiting other schools? New York is your home. You're a St. John's kid.' Then, he tells my mother, 'Other schools like to offer money, but we don't do that shit here. I could care less about letters of intent to other schools. If your son stands up and shakes my hand, that's it. He'll be here for four years, and I'll take care of him. He'll get his degree. I'll make sure of it.' Next thing you know, I'm on the phone calling [Oklahoma coach] Billy Tubbs, telling him that I'm sorry, but I'm going to St. John's. Man, Louie was like a gangster, but in a good way. You never wanted to disappoint him. I never met anyone like him in my life."

MICHAEL GRAHAM, GEORGETOWN: "Basketball wasn't really my thing, but it helped keep me out of trouble. I couldn't score, I couldn't shoot a free throw, but I could rebound and defend. My high school coach [Springarn's John Wood] had a beef with Coach Thompson, so he tried to steer me toward Maryland. But [Terrapins coach] Lefty Driesell had one of his assistants at my school almost every day, and I got sick of it. Then, I saw Patrick Ewing and [Virginia's] Ralph Sampson going at it, and how Georgetown lost to Memphis State [in the second round of the 1983 NCAA Tournament]. I don't want to sound cocky, but I knew I was the missing link. They needed a power forward, a tough guy to help Pat inside. Bill Martin was too small. At first I didn't have the grades to get into Georgetown, but I took summer courses through their Upward Bound program, and I got in."

EARL KELLEY, CONNECTICUT: "Everyone thought Syracuse had the inside track [on me], since my brother Larry played on their first Final Four team [in 1975]. I always played in his shadow, people saying I looked like him and talked like him. I wasn't sure I wanted to put up with the comparisons for another four years. I visited campus with Rafael Addison, and we were real tight from all the camps we went to. We both committed, but I wasn't gonna sign anything yet. I wanted to go home, tell my family, and show the other schools the respect they deserved by calling them to let them know I'd be going elsewhere. I told Boeheim that I'm coming, but that I wanted his word that no one will know until I officially sign. I got home from my trip in the middle of the week, and there was a story on the noon news about how I committed to Syracuse. I was so upset I called Coach Boeheim. He said he didn't know what happened, that one of his assistants must have leaked it. I told him that I just scratched Syracuse off my list, and hung up the phone on him. I thought he was playing me for a fool. Honest to God, before the sun set that day, I got a knock on my door, and it was Coach Boeheim. I believed he was sincere, and wasn't the one who let the cat out of the bag. But it was too late. I visited UConn a little later. I made my bones in that state, so I figured I'd stay for college."

BOBBY MARTIN, PITTSBURGH: "All five of my visits were to Big East schools, but I grew up in the shadow of Philadelphia and the Big Five. Rollie Massimino was a force of nature, and he told me that if I committed, he'd stop recruiting Perry Carter. Back then, I didn't think we could play together, which, now, is ridiculous. So I verballed to 'Nova. But Rollie never stopped recruiting Perry. I felt as though he lied to me. So I switched to Pitt, and after that, it wasn't pretty. Rollie only forgave me a few years ago. When I signed with Pitt, all my friends asked: 'How much [money] did they give you?' I'd say, 'Try nothing.' That was all because of the Doug West thing. Every time we played at 'Nova, the students there would jingle their car keys at me and throw fake dollar bills on the court."

ROGER MCCREADY, BOSTON COLLEGE: "I received some interest early on, but when Chris Mullin transferred to my high school [from Power Memorial], it all ballooned. I remember Gary Williams had been recruiting me hard at American, but I didn't want to go there. So I told him to please stop calling me, and I tried to be polite about it, but I guess I wasn't. I committed to B.C., when Dr. Tom [Davis] was the coach. But he left for Stanford, and Gary replaced him. Talk about small world. When Gary got the job, he called me and said, 'You blew me off before. What are you gonna do now?' I told him I still wanted to go to B.C., and he said, jokingly, 'I don't think I have a scholarship for you.' My host on my official visit there was [current Auburn coach] Bruce Pearl. He was a student-manager and sometimes filled in for the mascot."

DARREN MORNINGSTAR, PITTSBURGH: "I was 6-8 and only 185 pounds in high school, and even though my skill level was high, a lot of the major Division I schools didn't think I could guard an athlete on the wing or a bigger guy in the post. [Stanford coach] Mike Montgomery offered me a scholarship, but he took it off the table after Adam Keefe committed. All I know is that I wanted to go to a good academic school and one that would give me exposure, since my goal was to play in the NBA. Navy came into the picture when they started recruiting one of my AAU teammates. I knew nothing about the Naval Academy, other than it had just gone to the Elite Eight with David Robinson. I figured they got players of his caliber every year. Yeah, I was young and stupid. So I went to Navy, and I was completely unprepared for it. The Chesapeake Bay was beautiful, and I loved the surf and turf, but I had no idea what I was getting myself into. I was a fish out of water. Guys were there to become officers in the Navy, and I just wanted to play basketball. In one of my first games as a freshman, I had 20 points at [sixth-ranked] Iowa when they had B.J. Armstrong and Roy Marble, but I knew I wouldn't be around for long. I played five games before I decided to transfer. The coaching staff kind of steered me toward Pitt since a few of them were on [Panthers coach] Paul Evans's staff when he was at Navy. It ended up being a great move. Navy and Pitt were like night and day. Practices were the hardest part of my day at Pitt, but they were the easiest at Navy. I was in class with guys at Navy who had perfect SAT scores. I had a 3.96 GPA in high school, but these guys at Navy were ridiculously brilliant."

DARELLE PORTER, PITTSBURGH: "I grew up just a few blocks from [Pittsburgh's] Fitzgerald Field House, so when I became a Top 100 recruit and Pitt showed interest in me, I thought it was a natural fit. I didn't really entertain any other offers, but that didn't stop them from coming. It was a different type of world back then. There were no cell phones or beepers, and you had to pay a phone bill for long-distance calls. Staying home would allow me to get a home-cooked meal whenever I wanted. So I didn't have to incur a lot of the major expenses when you go away for college. But it got crazy before I officially signed. As a junior, I was getting letters from Canisius and [Division II] California [University of Pennsylvania], and was ecstatic about it. Then as a senior, I had Rick Pitino and [his assistants] Stu Jackson and Herb Sendek in my living room. And

Jim Calhoun paid a visit. Once word got out that you're a Big East recruit, then you quickly become a national recruit. I had [Arkansas's] Nolan Richardson and [Alabama's] Wimp Sanderson up to see me. Back then, you didn't have caller ID, so I let me buddies spend the night and answer the phone for me. There was never a question about where I was going."

DAVID RUSSELL, ST. JOHN'S: "It's funny. I didn't plan on going to college. I started getting letters as a junior, but I didn't take them too seriously. I never figured I'd be decent enough. But then I grew a few inches, and played well at Five-Star. All of a sudden, the whole Big East was recruiting me. I chose St. John's because of that Lou Carnesecca magic. I don't know what he said to me. I thought he was a funny little man who came to my house, but there was something about him that made you want to play for him."

RONY SEIKALY, SYRACUSE: "My older brother [Oscar Seikaly] played soccer at Colgate, and when I went to visit him one time when I was around 14, we went to a game at the Carrier Dome. We were sitting up in the nose-bleeds, and I was just amazed by everything. At one point, I turned to my brother, and said, 'I'm gonna play here one day.' He looked at me, and said, 'Well, you have a lot of work to do before that happens.' A couple of years later, I attended Coach Boeheim's camp, and at the end of it, he locked me in a room, and told me I wasn't leaving until I signed a letter of intent. That was pretty much it. I learned quickly that Coach was not a relationship guy. He didn't micromanage practice, and he didn't micromanage your life."

DICKEY SIMPKINS, PROVIDENCE: "I grew up in the DMV [D.C./ Maryland/Virginia region], and all I watched was Big East and ACC basketball. Later on in my career, when I played with the Bulls, I used to joke with Bill Wennington [St. John's] that I used to watch him on TV when I was in sixth grade. I remember back in ninth grade I wore a Patrick Ewing jersey on my first day of high school. This was back in 1986, when no one was wearing jerseys, but I was rocking a Pat Ewing with those high-top Nikes that Georgetown used to wear. I would've liked to go to Maryland, because I was a big Lefty [Driesell] fan. But after Len Bias died, he left. And Big John [Thompson] didn't start recruiting me until the tail end, when I had my mind made up on Providence. I was a different breed. I wanted to go somewhere where I could help build something, where I could start right away and make my own name. Providence checked off all my boxes. PC basketball is the biggest thing in Rhode Island. The school didn't have a football team, and it was small, so I wouldn't get lost in the mix. Plus, they played in a big arena. Coach [Rick] Barnes was a closer, and had a type of pizzazz with how he talked to players. He sold me on all those things. Yeah, Providence didn't have that cosmetic appeal that most kids looked for, but Coach Barnes made you feel like you were a part of something special. Even Tim Duncan came on an official visit my senior year."

**WHAT WAS YOUR "WELCOME TO THE BIG EAST" MOMENT
WHEN IT BECAME CLEAR THAT YOU WERE
NOW PLAYING IN A MAN'S LEAGUE?**

ABDUL ABDULLAH, PROVIDENCE: "I remember Coach Barnes had us fill out index cards. We had to write down what we thought our role was. He said, 'I'll let you know whether or not you're correct.' Nowadays, coaches could never get away with coaching like that, restricting players from doing certain things. He literally told some players to never shoot. He'd say, 'You can't shoot. What the hell are you doing?' That was new to me. I didn't mind it, because we were successful doing it his way. My big men ran the floor like greyhounds, and I enjoyed rewarding their faith in me."

MARQUES BRAGG, PROVIDENCE: "Eric [Murdock] and I used to wrestle each other all the time. He was one year older than me, but I was always stronger than him. Until after he had a year of the Big East under his belt. I remember messing around with him, and he was so much bigger. And he was just a point guard. That's when I realized what I was in for as an interior player."

JOEY BROWN, GEORGETOWN: "Mine happened in practice. Alonzo Mourning was so competitive. I always prided myself on playing hard, but 'Zo's intensity level was something I'd never seen in my life. It didn't matter if it was a shooting drill or a layup line. He did it 110 percent, straight business. I'd call my friends at home, and say, 'Yo, Alonzo is a madman!' Dude was scary when he was dialed in."

BRYAN CAVER, SETON HALL: "We were playing Pitt, and I was chasing Sean Miller. He cut through the lane, and I was watching the ball out on the wing. Brian Shorter hit me like I've never been hit before. Oh, man, I had a bruised sternum, and my chest hurt for like three weeks. I learned really fast to keep my head on a swivel, especially if I went in the paint."

BILL CURLEY, BOSTON COLLEGE: "When I got there, I was one of four freshman starters. We beat Providence in our first Big East game and didn't win another one the rest of the season. Everyone stomped on us. We finished 1-15 in the conference. Welcome to the Big East."

TERRY DEHERE, SETON HALL: "I was a freshman playing Georgetown at the Cap Centre [in Landover, Md.]. When I saw John Thompson walk out of the tunnel, I couldn't believe how big he was. I'd seen him before on TV, but never realized just how tall he was. I was so scared. On our first three possessions, we had three straight three-second violations in the paint. We couldn't even get a shot up."

ERIC EBERZ, VILLANOVA: "I wish I would've redshirted my freshman year, because I barely played. It took some time to adjust to how fast and physical the Big East was. It took me a while to hit my stride."

PHIL GAMBLE, CONNECTICUT: "My freshman year, [Boston College senior] Dom Pressley dunked on me, and said, 'Welcome to the Big East.' I mean, he dunked right in my face."

OTIS HILL, SYRACUSE: "I was always a rugged guy, having played football, and I prided myself on having heart. But when we played against Providence when I was a freshman, I got so beat up. Michael Smith and Dickey Simpkins were bruisers, and they knocked me down the whole game. They were both cool with Lawrence Moten, because they were all from that D.C./Baltimore area, and afterward, they told him that they thought I was gonna be a lot tougher than that. Lawrence told me, I think, because he knew it would motivate me. It sure did, because I always circled Providence on the schedule after that. I gave them the business more than once."

JEROME LANE, PITTSBURGH: "Mine was against Georgetown in one of my first conference games. Ralph Dalton knocked me so hard to the ground [that] I couldn't believe it. I complained to the ref, and he said, 'You better get up and keep playing. That's nothing compared to what you're getting into.' Man, I was so scared to go in the paint after that."

JASON LAWSON, VILLANOVA: "As a freshman, two of my earliest Big East games were against Providence and Boston College. One night, I was fighting for position against Dickey Simpkins and Michael Smith. The next, I was banging against Bill Curley and Danya Abrams. Physically, they just wore on me. I said, 'Yo, this league is no joke!' I fouled out almost half my games that year."

JOHN LINEHAN, PROVIDENCE: "Mine was literally a 'Welcome to the Big East' moment. It was a practice early in my freshman year, when they had just come off that Elite Eight appearance. I remember struggling to bring the ball up the court against Corey Wright, because he was so strong. Finally, I got past half-court, and drove to the basket. Jamel Thomas was waiting there, and hit me with a forearm to the chest that sent me flying. He looked at me, and said, 'Welcome to the Big East, rookie.'"

JERRY MCCULLOUGH, PITTSBURGH: "Alonzo Mourning introduced me to the conference. When I was a freshman, Coach [Paul] Evans put me in late in the game against Georgetown to break their press. The plan was for me to get in the lane and dish it off to the open man. I figured that this was my moment to prove that Alonzo was no big deal, since all you ever heard back then was noise about this dude. So I got the ball, dribbled through the press, and made it to the paint. I went up, drew contact, put my shoulder into his chest, and he punched the ball out of bounds. Coach gave me hell for that one."

DARREN MORNINGSTAR, PITTSBURGH: "Sitting out my transfer year helped me physically, but there's really nothing that can prepare you for the Big East. One time against Georgetown, I popped out to the elbow to catch a pass, and Alonzo Mourning lunged for the steal and missed it. So I turn and have an open path to the basket. This was in front of Georgetown's bench, and I could see John Thompson in my periphery. I'm thinking, 'I'm gonna dunk the shit out of this!' I take one dribble and cock back to hammer it, and out of nowhere on the weak side, Dikembe Mutombo comes and swipes it out of my hand like a windshield wiper. John Thompson yelled, 'Get that shit outta here!'"

JAY MURPHY, BOSTON COLLEGE: "The minute I stepped foot on campus. I thought of myself as a midlevel recruit, and truth be told, I didn't know my ass from my elbow. A few seniors came in 20 pounds overweight during the fall of my freshman year, and Dr. Tom [Davis] wasn't having it. So, by hook or by crook, I ended up starting right away. I was very lucky. I played with two guards [John Bagley and Michael Adams] who were less than six feet tall, who ended up playing more than 20 years combined in the NBA. I was really the beneficiary of them."

JOHN PINONE, VILLANOVA: "When Rollie was recruiting me, he fawned all over me. He'd tell me how special of a player I was, how I was going to do this, how I was going to do that. Then practice started my freshman year, and he didn't even know my name. I was just a number. Nowadays, the NCAA has rules restricting how much teams can practice, but back then, we'd go 13 straight days without a day off. And we went hard every day. I remember we practiced for like three hours the Wednesday night before Thanksgiving, had off on Thanksgiving, then practiced at noon on Friday. Rollie would say to us, 'What are you guys complaining about? I just gave you three days off!' He didn't want to be just good; he wanted to be great."

DARELLE PORTER, PITTSBURGH: "It was against Syracuse. We had this play, where Jerome Lane would come set a down screen for me, and I'd pop out to the wing. I'd get open 90 percent of the time, because Jerome was a beast and would just pin my man. This time, [Syracuse's] Earl Duncan put an arm bar on me, and I couldn't move. I mean that literally—I could not move. I said to myself, 'Damn, this is some grown-man stuff. I better get in the weight room if I'm gonna go to war in this league.'"

SHAWNELLE SCOTT, ST. JOHN'S: "Two things I'll never forget my freshman year. The first was against Georgetown, when Robert Werdann was hurt, and I had to guard Dikembe Mutombo and Alonzo Mourning. In my mind, I had to block out the magnitude of what I was doing. The second was going to Syracuse with 30,000 fans screaming in the Carrier Dome, and Billy Owens whispering to me, 'You in trouble.'"

RONY SEIKALY, SYRACUSE: "I graduated high school early in December [1983], so I was fortunate enough to join the team as a redshirt in January. Those two, three months helped me a lot. At the banquet before the Big East Tournament, I was seated next to Patrick Ewing. I was just in awe of this legend. I thought he'd be the meanest guy in the world, but it turned out he was the nicest. That niceness didn't extend to the court, though."

CHRIS SMITH, CONNECTICUT: "For me, going against Georgetown and their Eiffel Towers [Mutombo and Mourning] was quite the eye-opener. Getting into the lane was easy, but getting a shot off over top of them was almost impossible."

JERRY WALKER, SETON HALL: "Playing at home against Georgetown and Alonzo Mourning as a freshman. I had a fractured wrist, and they wanted to redshirt me, but I didn't want to. I entered the game as the sixth man, and the crowd was really cheering for me. Alonzo said, 'They really like you here, huh? Well, I'm gonna show them why they shouldn't.' I told him to meet me in the tunnel after the game."

DESCRIBE WHAT LIFE WAS LIKE IN THE BIG EAST.

DANYA ABRAMS, BOSTON COLLEGE: "When you had to bang against [Villanova's] Chuck Kornegay, [Providence's] Dickey Simpkins, and [Connecticut's] Donyell Marshall, every game was a dogfight. There were no two-minute interviews and out of the locker room after the game. It was ice bags and guys slumped on the floor."

SCOTT BURRELL, CONNECTICUT: "A lot of college basketball teams back then had names without games. In the Big East, they had names and the games to go along with it."

ROBERT CHURCHWELL, GEORGETOWN: "For me, there was a huge adjustment to life under John Thompson. From his point of view, it was a business, point blank, where you were essentially getting paid—room and board, books, and tuition—to play at a high level. When I was a freshman, we were playing Houston down in Tampa, and it was probably one of my best games early on. I was at the back of our press and was exhausted, so I put my hand up, asking for a breather. On the next possession, I got a reverse dunk. And when I was running back down the floor, Coach was screaming at me, 'Your ass ain't tired! If you can dunk, you don't need a sub!' That's what it was like every day."

STEVEN EDWARDS, MIAMI: "As a competitor, you can be star-struck for a second—and believe me, I was—but then you get hit in the chest and realize it's time to play."

BILLY GOODWIN, ST. JOHN'S: "It was heaven. For my teammates who were from New York City, you had a choice. You could live at home, and pocket most of the stipend you got for living expenses. Or you could get your own place with the money. A lot of guys stayed home. Not me. I got an apartment in Jamaica Estates. It was the first place I ever lived that had a doorman. Life was good."

MALCOLM HUCKABY, BOSTON COLLEGE: "Physical. You could hand-check, you could bump, you could bang. Everything but a fistfight. For three years [1989-92], the Big East experimented by allowing a sixth foul in conference play. I entered college 165 pounds, and I left at 215."

JAREN JACKSON, GEORGETOWN: "Our practices summed it up to me. There were times when we wouldn't even touch a ball. Coach [Thompson] had his famous chair, and he'd plop it down, and just sit there. He'd simply move his finger or blow his whistle. 'Keep running!' You had no idea when it would stop, no idea what someone did wrong to warrant all that running. He'd giggle and laugh at us. You could tell he got a big kick out of it. We're all upset, dying for a break, begging for water. And Coach would say, 'I'm gonna run the shit outta you!' Then, he'd start laughing again. We had a lot of athletes, and were a full-court team. But the amount of running we did … damn!"

FELIPE LOPEZ, ST. JOHN'S: "It was tough trying to find our way. Louie [Carnesecca] was an icon and had an established way of doing things. He had a recipe for success that lasted for almost 30 years. It was hard to duplicate that, playing for two different head coaches [Brian Mahoney and Fran Fraschilla]. It was hard, finding an identity."

ANDRE MCCLOUD, SETON HALL: "The coaches' antics summed it up. They were entertaining in their own, personal way. You had John Thompson and Rollie Massimino going at it, and John Thompson wearing a sweater to tease Lou Carnesecca."

DARREN MORNINGSTAR, PITTSBURGH: "Every team was dirty. You knew you were gonna get popped when the refs weren't looking. One time against St. John's, I was guarding Jayson Williams, and he had a wide-open look. I tried to foul him, but I ended up raking his eyes. Man, he was pissed. He started chasing me all over the Garden, and they gave him a technical foul. [Teammate] Jason Matthews comes up to me and says, 'Star, what the hell are you doing?' I said, 'What do you mean? You're going to the line to shoot free throws. You're welcome.'"

MIKE MOSES, ST. JOHN'S: "Bully ball. Even in practice. The year I sat out [after my transfer], I think it took me a month and a half to score on [teammate] Kevin Williams. When I became eligible, I remember playing Georgetown. Bill Wennington took off his jersey after the game, and he was covered in red welts and bruises. I said, 'What the hell happened to you?' He said, 'Patrick Ewing, man. His elbows are brutal.' It made you long for the nonconference games we had at the beginning of the season."

JAY MURPHY, BOSTON COLLEGE: "Back then, every game was played in a bandbox. Except for the Carrier Dome, every school's gym was tiny and smelled of sweat. Every home court was worth at least a half-dozen points."

CONSTANTIN POPA, MIAMI: "With all due respect to today's Big East, there's no comparison to what the league was like back then. It was rough. We got rocked left and right. Every year, we'd get off to a decent start, but once conference play started, everything went south."

DAVID RUSSELL, ST. JOHN'S: "If you weren't ready, you'd get blown off the floor. You couldn't sleep on anyone. The competition was that stiff. Coach [Carnesecca] used to say, 'You better put on your boxing gloves, because this one's going 12 rounds.' He knew what he was talking about, because your jersey would be soaked in sweat and blood by the end of the night."

DICKEY SIMPKINS, PROVIDENCE: "There was absolutely no learning curve for a young big man. Post play in the Big East was so strong; everything was so accelerated. Pitt had Brian Shorter, who we used to call an ox. Syracuse was athletic with Conrad McRae and LeRon Ellis. And Georgetown was just long with Dikembe and Alonzo. Their elbows were lethal."

JOHN WALLACE, SYRACUSE: "It was beautiful. A lot of guys were envious of the freedom that Coach Boeheim gave us. No other coach in the conference was letting their four or five bring the ball up the court and shoot 3s. When I hear all the praise given to Coach, I don't hear enough about how good of a motivator he was. He was a tremendous confidence-builder. He made you believe you were the best player on the court, and you never took a bad shot."

ROBERT WERDANN, ST. JOHN'S: "We approached basketball like we were professionals, in terms of the time we either spent on the court or in preparation. Coach [Carnesecca] always said that he would treat us like pros. That's great, but the thing was, we were still students. Guys would always fall asleep in study hall, because they were so physically and mentally drained."

WHO WAS THE HARDEST PLAYER TO DEFEND?

ABDUL ABDULLAH, PROVIDENCE: "Jerry McCullough. He was one of the few guards in the Big East who had the freedom to go one on one any time he wanted. He was the ultimate freelancer."

RAFAEL ADDISON, SYRACUSE: "There were a lot of great players from my era who didn't get the credit they deserved, because they were overshadowed by bigger names [like Patrick Ewing and Chris Mullin]. It's impossible to narrow it down. Otis Thorpe from Providence was one. [Pittsburgh's] Clyde Vaughan was a monster at the small forward position. And I had some great battles with [Georgetown's] Reggie Williams and David Wingate. They were a lot like me, in terms of being interchangeable. They were from Baltimore and were a product of a major inner-city. We all had similar mentalities."

DONNY BROWN, PROVIDENCE: "[Syracuse's] Pearl Washington. He was 6-2, strong as an ox, and built like a seal. He could maneuver anywhere on the court. If you bumped him, you felt like you were bumping into a wall. You couldn't hand-check him, either, because he wouldn't even feel it. Overall, though, the most talented player I faced was Earl Kelley. We were cool. When we were freshmen, we shared the same bus traveling to the Big East Tournament, and we ended up sitting next to each other. Imagine that today—two teams sharing the same bus."

FRED BROWN, GEORGETOWN: "[Teammate] Sleepy Floyd. He had so much speed with the ball, and knew how to get free without it."

JOEY BROWN, GEORGETOWN: "Bryan Caver. He was so underrated. He was 6-4 and had long arms. I personally thought he went to the wrong school. For as great as a coach P.J. Carlesimo was, he ran nothing but half-court sets, and I always thought of Bryan as more of an open-court player. Chris Smith was tough. So was [Providence's] Eric Murdock, because he was always squared up to the basket. He torched me so bad one game that I went back to my room in tears. Literally, I was crying."

SCOTT BURRELL, CONNECTICUT: "Malik Sealy worked me out. He gave me my first lesson in the Big East. He was quick, athletic, and could shoot the midrange jumper. And he moved along the baseline so well."

BRYAN CAVER, SETON HALL: "Chris Smith and Sean Miller. Chris was unbelievably strong and could really handle the ball, and Sean wasn't fast, but he was so knowledgeable. It's no wonder he became a great coach [at Xavier and Arizona]."

TERRY DEHERE, SETON HALL: "Lance Miller was a tough cover. He was quirky, really herky-jerky, and smart with the ball. Billy Owens was difficult when Syracuse spread the floor. He was dangerous out of their four corners. And Jason Matthews was a guy you could never leave alone. He was automatic."

STEVEN EDWARDS, MIAMI: "Lawrence Moten. He wasn't fast. I compare him to [Hall of Fame wide receiver] Steve Largent. Steve knew how to run routes and understood the game. That's how Lawrence was. He had such a high basketball I.Q. and knew how to score every way possible. Sometimes it was like looking at him in slow motion."

PHIL GAMBLE, CONNECTICUT: "[Boston College's] Dana Barros. He was so quick, and could shoot from so far out. In high school, he played three different sports, and was such a great athlete. He had the attitude to go with it, too. We couldn't check him, so we played a box-and-one on him a lot."

BILLY GOODWIN, ST. JOHN'S: "John Bagley and [Georgetown's] Sleepy Floyd. Bagley had the whole package. He had such a strong upper body, and could move you in so many ways. He could finish against anyone. And Sleepy could shoot the lights out, even out to 30 feet. So you had to body him up, but he was so quick off the dribble."

OTIS HILL, SYRACUSE: "[Georgetown's] Othella Harrington. For one, he was left-handed, and that's always different. We had a strange, personal rivalry that started at the Nike/ABCD camp when we were still in high school. He and Jason Kidd were the top-ranked recruits in the country, and I played pretty well against them. Ever since, Othella and I brought out the best in each other."

MALCOLM HUCKABY, BOSTON COLLEGE: "Kerry Kittles. Like Tayshaun Prince, he wasn't bulky, but he was deceptively strong. He was a gazelle in the open court. One time, Bill Curley and I tried to trap him high on the wing, to force him to get rid of the ball. But he split us, and took off for this monster dunk."

KERRY KITTLES, VILLANOVA: "Lawrence Moten was so unpredictable. He was smooth and silky, and didn't waste any movement."

JEROME LANE, PITTSBURGH: "[Seton Hall's] Ramon Ramos. He was stronger than I thought and could score better than I thought. He never got enough credit for how good he was."

JASON LAWSON, VILLANOVA: "Shawnelle Scott knew how to use his body to get position. He was older and crafty, and always seemed to get the benefit of the call. Othella Harrington was tough, too, because he was left-handed and had that flicky shot you couldn't block. He had quick feet and could face up."

JOHN LINEHAN, PROVIDENCE: "[Connecticut's] Khalid El-Amin and [Boston College's] Troy Bell. El-Amin was the toughest guard to figure out. He was so crafty with the ball, and had deceptive speed. He'd go from slow to quick in the blink of an eye. And Troy could flat-out score."

FELIPE LOPEZ, ST. JOHN'S: "[Georgetown's] Allen Iverson, no doubt. It was a challenge because he had no conscience; he had the neon light. Not the green light—that's for regular players. He had the neon light."

BOBBY MARTIN, PITTSBURGH: "Other than [teammate] Brian Shorter [in practice], I'd have to say Malik Sealy. He was always moving, always running off a pick that you had to fight through."

JERRY MCCULLOUGH, PITTSBURGH: "No one. I can't give anyone credit for that. That's my ego. Whether or not a guy scored on me, in my mind, I shut him down."

LANCE MILLER, VILLANOVA: "I would say my cousin, Eric Murdock, but that wouldn't count. You weren't even allowed to touch him. He'd go to the free-throw line like 20 times a game. Billy Owens was the hardest to defend. He could shoot, go to the hole, or post up—there was nothing he couldn't do. You had to be on him all night. It wasn't that he'd go off for 30 points; it's just that he'd have 20 points, 12 boards, and seven assists, and you'd be wondering what the hell happened."

DARREN MORNINGSTAR, PITTSBURGH: "Derrick Coleman. Big guys who could shoot like that drew you 25 feet from the basket. Shawn Kemp was like that when I guarded him in the pros. For as difficult as it was to defend Shaq and Alonzo, at least you knew where they were going to be."

LAWRENCE MOTEN, SYRACUSE: "There were two. Kerry Kittles was like guarding Reggie Miller. He never got tired. He'd run you for days. If you weren't physically ready to go for 40 minutes, he'd give you hell coming off screens. And then [Connecticut's] Ray Allen. I'm not talking about the Ray Allen of the Celtics or Miami, the spot-up shooter. I'm talking about the Jesus Shuttlesworth version, the one who'd take you off the dribble and dunk on you. The Ray Allen of the Milwaukee Bucks."

JAY MURPHY, BOSTON COLLEGE: "[Pittsburgh's] Clyde Vaughan was one hell of a player."

JOHN PINONE, VILLANOVA: "Besides Patrick Ewing, I'd say Danny Schayes [Syracuse] and Jay Murphy. Jay was long and lanky and could draw you away from the basket, where it's uncomfortable for most big men."

DARELLE PORTER, PITTSBURGH: "Billy Owens. I've guarded everyone from [6-10] Derrick Coleman to [Seton Hall's 5-3] Pookey Wigington. Billy could do it all. Plus, he was strong enough to absorb your most physical defense. My first encounter with him was in high school. I was a sophomore, and he was a freshman, and his team beat mine for the state championship. I knew he'd be special."

DAVID RUSSELL, ST. JOHN'S: "[Boston College's] John Garris. He was big, he was strong, and he could play 15 feet from the rim."

RONY SEIKALY, SYRACUSE: "Patrick Ewing. Even though we played mostly zone, his sheer dominance—his size and the way he played above the rim—was overwhelming."

DICKEY SIMPKINS, PROVIDENCE: "Donyell Marshall. He was a perimeter-oriented big man who could put it on the floor. They ran everything through him, which meant he was gonna touch the ball on every possession."

JERRY WALKER, SETON HALL: "For me, it wasn't Alonzo Mourning. I knew how to use angles, and leverage my lower center of gravity to push him off the block. I'd say Billy Owens was my most difficult matchup. He had kind of an awkward game, where he'd jump off the wrong leg. It was unorthodox, but it was effective."

JOHN WALLACE, SYRACUSE: "It was always the big men who weren't getting the ball on offense, who were so hungry that they'd beat you to the offensive glass. Jerry Walker, [Providence's] Michael Smith, and Lamont Middleton [of St. John's]—you couldn't game-plan for them."

ROBERT WERDANN, ST. JOHN'S: "Ramon Ramos. He wasn't as tall as me, but he was an immovable object as far as I was concerned."

DOUG WEST, VILLANOVA: "[Georgetown's] Reggie Williams, by far. He was a legit 6-8, and had a great stroke and post-up game. And he ran the floor so well. Our personal battles continued for years in the NBA."

JEROME WILLIAMS, GEORGETOWN: "John Wallace. He was a scorer-galore. He had an array of offensive moves at the four spot, and could nail it from deep. [Providence's] Austin Croshere was another formidable forward. Dude was a problem child."

> ## NOW THAT YOU'RE OUT OF THE MEDIA'S SPOTLIGHT, AND NO LONGER HAVE TO WORRY ABOUT YOUR COMMENTS ENDING UP ON ANOTHER TEAM'S BULLETIN BOARD, WHAT OPPONENT DID YOU HATE THE MOST?

DANYA ABRAMS, BOSTON COLLEGE: "I hated UConn, and it wasn't a regional thing. They were the pretty boys of the Big East. They all had nice fades and Nike gear, while we were stuck with Starter and Reebok. They always brought out the best in us. Every game was close—overtimes, double overtimes—but they always found a way to beat us."

RAFAEL ADDISON, SYRACUSE: "I'd have to say St. John's. The students there were on you. If I had a bad game, they'd say I was on drugs, and I'm clean as a whistle. Nothing was off-limits. Plus, they had Chris Mullin. Outside, he had that look like he could be playing a guitar with The Beatles, but inside, he wanted to take your heart out."

MARQUES BRAGG, PROVIDENCE: "We weren't rivals with anyone back then. People didn't think we were good enough to be considered on equal footing. UConn was so cocky, and with Seton Hall being the team in my backyard, it was always personal with them."

SCOTT BURRELL, CONNECTICUT: "Georgetown. They were the dirtiest team in the league. Every game was a dogfight, no matter who was on their team. You'd be so sore after playing them. And I can't leave out Syracuse with their big dome and their bright orange swag. Syracuse seemed like a reminder of what we didn't have. For us, Coach Calhoun would come in wearing a nice, new sweatsuit. And he'd say, 'You guys like this? Well, you ain't getting them until you do something.'"

TERRY DEHERE, SETON HALL: "Georgetown. They teetered on that line between dirty and not dirty. Even if I was away from the ball, standing in the corner, I'd still somehow get punched in the stomach."

ERIC EBERZ, VILLANOVA: "I didn't like UConn. Maybe it was a jealousy thing, because they were so good. Maybe it was because we always got snowed in when we went up there. So, in my sophomore year, when I hit the 3 with 2.1 seconds left to beat them at the [du Pont] Pavilion, it was the greatest feeling in the world. I think that was the last time Villanova played a Top 5 opponent on campus, and the crowd was nuts."

EARL KELLEY, CONNECTICUT: "Georgetown. And it had nothing to do with their physical brand of ball. I was fit for that. Was I scared of Patrick Ewing? Come on. I remember him at camp when he was 13, and wore a pair of Converse with his toes sticking out. Dudes were picking on him. Here's what made me mad about Georgetown: They were sore losers. I was always taught to be graceful in victory and defeat. When they won, they hung around on the court, smiling and whooping it up. Not rubbing it in, just celebrating. But when they lost, they'd pile up, turn their backs on you, and retreat to the locker room. You can have that us-against-the-world mentality. But if you know someone, you can't communicate with them? I mean, people were calling Ewing a monkey. Let the man talk. Let the man express himself. And another reason: Not one of their guards was better than me, and I proved it every time we played them."

JEROME LANE, PITTSBURGH: "Georgetown. We fought them twice in one season. That's the reason they instituted mandatory suspensions for fighting."

JASON LAWSON, VILLANOVA: "Pitt. Their students did everything but throw coins at us."

FELIPE LOPEZ, ST. JOHN'S: "I hated UConn. They had a little more swag than most teams. They had a cockiness about themselves I just didn't like, especially Ray Allen and Richard Hamilton. I wanted to kick their ass."

BOBBY MARTIN, PITTSBURGH: "Seton Hall. They had Mark Bryant and Ramon Ramos. The Big East was physical enough, but they took it to another level. They used to give us fits."

JASON MATTHEWS, PITTSBURGH: "Georgetown. They used to foul on every play. Every single play for four years. It's the truth. Part of my redemption against them was when I would hit a 3, Alonzo would get so mad. He'd start fussing out his guards for not forcing me to drive into him and Dikembe. Go back and look at the tapes. The look on Alonzo's face was priceless."

DWAYNE MCCLAIN, VILLANOVA: "Syracuse. The dome threw everything off. You put a basketball court in the middle of a football field, and it's going to screw up your depth perception. Plus, no one wants to go to Syracuse in the winter. It's cold as hell up there."

ROGER MCCREADY, BOSTON COLLEGE: "Georgetown. Fights were commonplace. You expected it when you played them. And I'm not talking about the normal bumping and elbowing that goes on underneath the basket. They'd get right up in your face, so you just had to get in theirs."

MIKE MOSES, ST. JOHN'S: "Syracuse. They thought that since they had that big, shiny dome, they could come into New York City and sign any player they wanted. That bothered me."

JAY MURPHY, BOSTON COLLEGE: "Connecticut, our next-door neighbors. We had four starters who were from Connecticut: John Bagley, Michael Adams, John Garris, and myself. So our games with UConn took on extra meaning. And I'd like to add that we were 7-1 against them when I played."

CONSTANTIN POPA, MIAMI: "Pittsburgh. I never wanted to go there. It was cold and gray in the winter, and the atmosphere in their gym was crazy. The bleachers were so close to the backboard, and the students were nuts."

DARELLE PORTER, PITTSBURGH: "St. John's. For some reason, the players there always tried to pick on [teammate] Sean Miller. And the students there were brutal. They'd call him a porn star, because he had a thin mustache. When you played St. John's at Alumni Hall [now Carnesecca Arena], the students were on top of you. And they did their research. One year, some of our recruits couldn't qualify academically, so they'd chant stuff about the SAT and how we couldn't read."

DAVID RUSSELL, ST. JOHN'S: "Georgetown, by far. I don't know what John Thompson said to them before their games, but they'd all come out with hate in their systems. They were foaming at the mouth by the time they took the floor."

SHAWNELLE SCOTT, ST. JOHN'S: "I'm from New York. I hated everybody. I didn't like Connecticut, Syracuse, Seton Hall, and especially Georgetown. They were all great cultures, and everyone in the conference had an attitude, that chip on their shoulder. You couldn't sleep on anybody. When January came around, there were no smiles, no room for error."

RONY SEIKALY, SYRACUSE: "Georgetown. We didn't like their attitude and that whole intimidation factor. John Thompson would be on the sidelines with that big towel trying to scare the refs. It was their whole demeanor, even their black uniforms. Everyone else in the conference is wearing bright colors—orange or blue—and they wore dark colors."

DICKEY SIMPKINS, PROVIDENCE: "Boston College and UConn. B.C. ran all these offensive sets for Bill Curley, and he used to get so many touches. And that made me mad because my team didn't really feature me like that offensively. And against UConn, we were winning by a point at home my senior year with like eight seconds left, and Kevin Ollie drove the length of the floor and scored with about two seconds left to give them the win. Man, I was super-hot."

CHRIS SMITH, CONNECTICUT: "I hated playing Villanova. We liked to get out and run, but they always found a way to slow the game down with a zone."

JOHN WALLACE, SYRACUSE: "Playing at Syracuse, you're programmed to hate Georgetown. From our standpoint, we're all cool dudes who like to hang out. But the Georgetown guys were all uptight. Aside from Allen Iverson and Jerome Williams, who I'm good friends with today, every Georgetown player seemed like a robot. And I'd like to point out that we dominated them in my four years, so fuck 'em."

DOUG WEST, VILLANOVA: "Pitt. The students there were relentless, because I went public with the doctor offering me all that money to go there. They printed these big checks, made out to me for $10,000 and ZERO SENSE, and waved them at me all game. When we played there, I had to stay on a different floor of the hotel than my teammates, and have a bodyguard outside the door. I had a police escort everywhere I went. I remember my teammates joking that I had to run out on the court first, in case there was a sniper in the stands who wanted to pick me off."

> IN HIGH SCHOOL, YOU COULD SINGLE-HANDEDLY CARRY YOUR TEAM
> TO SUCCESS. SO IT'S FAIR TO SAY THAT YOU EXPERIENCED NOTHING
> BUT SUCCESS AS A TEENAGER. OBVIOUSLY, COLLEGE BASKETBALL
> ISN'T LIKE THAT. WHAT WAS IT LIKE TO DEAL WITH LOSING?

DONNY BROWN, PROVIDENCE: "Even though the standings might say you're on the bottom, you don't really feel like that. You went to practice and worked hard, and we all felt like we were a recruit away from rising up to the top. We entered every game believing we could win. We never adopted that loser mentality. It helped you gain perspective. We were the lucky one percent that were fortunate enough to play in the Big East. It took so much out of you just to compete in that conference that you never talked about being on the bottom."

BILL CURLEY, BOSTON COLLEGE: "I ultimately chose B.C. [over Connecticut] because I was intrigued by the prospect of helping to change the culture. It had been a beat-down program for a while, and I wanted that challenge. But it proved to be a lot harder than I thought."

STEVEN EDWARDS, MIAMI: "It was a learning process, for sure. Nobody gets used to losing. It can do one of two things: It can fracture your team, or make it come closer together. It made us tighter. Coach Ham did a good job of motivating kids who'd never been in a losing program before. It's hard to get players up for practice when they're losing."

PHIL GAMBLE, CONNECTICUT: "It was an adjustment. Fans in the Hartford Civic Center would wear bags over their heads. You could say losing broadened my horizon, since it made me lazy off the court, and I learned some hard lessons. Cliff Robinson and I missed 15 games our sophomore year because of academic issues. Some students would drive by us, and call us dummies. But we also got a lot of encouragement. My mother, she didn't have much, but she would send me a care package with those Little Debbie oatmeal pies. It meant the world to me. Things changed immediately when Coach Calhoun was hired, though."

MALCOLM HUCKABY, BOSTON COLLEGE: "I lost only six games in my four years of high school, and none as a senior when we won the state championship. So losing in college was humbling. It seemed like every team in the Big East had a lottery pick. Looking back, it was the right way to build. You bring in a class, and let them take their licks as freshmen. You give them time to develop and grow, and you monitor their progression. Nowadays, you don't see that often."

EARL KELLEY, CONNECTICUT: "I knew it wouldn't be easy, but being the type of player I was, I always thought the next game would be the one. That's what drove me. We never went to practice with our heads down. Losing hurt more when I was away from the court than when I was on it. We'd watch other teams on TV, and we knew we were just as good as them. We just had to stop making a little mistake here or a little mistake there. You start wondering what the problem is. Is it me? But that's just your mind messing with you. In four years, I can count on one hand the times when we were blown out. I love my alma mater, but all those banners hanging in the rafters of Gampel [Pavilion] came on my back. Guys like me, Corny Thompson, Karl Hobbs, Tim Coles, Norm Bailey—we inspired other players to come."

ANDRE MCCLOUD, SETON HALL: "Every time I went out there, I felt that I had to prove I belonged, that my statistics were no joke, even though we weren't winning that much. It was hard to handle losing—very hard—but I kept telling myself that we were building for the next generation. There were a lot of guys who couldn't handle the situation and left, but I told P.J. [Carlesimo] that I started this, so I'm gonna finish it. When I saw how far John Morton and Ramon Ramos and all the others had come in order to get to the [1989 NCAA Tournament] final, I definitely felt a sense of ownership in that. When they were freshman and I was a senior, I saw all the ups and downs they had trying to learn the game. That was special to see much they'd grown. If I had to do it all over again, I'd still go to Seton Hall."

LANCE MILLER, VILLANOVA: "It actually wasn't as difficult as you'd expect. We competed every night, and the better teams had multiple NBA players. That was usually the difference. Plus, we were in a transitional period. Rollie Massimino was testing out his new chuck-and-duck philosophy that allowed us to press and play up-tempo. It was new for him to put the chips on the table, and just let it fly. So we could beat anybody, but lose to anybody. I think we lost to a team that only had two wins."

**WHO WAS THE BIGGEST TRASH-TALKER
DURING YOUR TIME IN THE CONFERENCE?**

ABDUL ABDULLAH, PROVIDENCE: "[Connecticut's] Donny Marshall. He was like their team spokesman, and would never shut the fuck up. He'd be hooting and hollering: 'We're gonna beat the shit out of these guys! These fucking guys aren't on our level!' I'll tell you one guy who was Donny's opposite and never said a word: Kerry Kittles. He was an absolute assassin. We'd try to engage him, but he'd be stone silent."

RAFAEL ADDISON, SYRACUSE: "Anyone from Georgetown. Pick one. They were bad boys like the Oakland Raiders or the Detroit Pistons back then. I can't leave out Earl Kelley, though. He was the ultimate trash-talker, but he backed it up."

DONNY BROWN, PROVIDENCE: "[Georgetown's] Michael Jackson. There was one dead-ball situation. I think it was a free throw, and we were both standing at half-court. He said to me, 'West Coast basketball ain't shit!' I bumped him and the ref broke it up, but, man, I was ready to go. I told him, 'You know, if I was playing with Pat Ewing, I'd be twice the guard you are.'"

FRED BROWN, GEORGETOWN: "No one talked trash to me. They knew that if they did, I'd knock their ass out!"

JOEY BROWN, GEORGETOWN: "Terry Dehere talked a lot of noise, and so did basically everyone at Syracuse."

SCOTT BURRELL, CONNECTICUT: "Alonzo Mourning was big, strong, tough, and he never stopped talking."

ROBERT CHURCHWELL, GEORGETOWN: "Charles Minlend from St. John's always ran his mouth. Terry Dehere yapped a lot, too."

TERRY DEHERE, SETON HALL: "Me. That's the Jersey in me. That's just how you grew up in the playgrounds, always cracking jokes. I always felt that if you were playing without talking trash, you weren't really playing. When it came time to jump ball, I'd ask the other team who drew the assignment [of guarding me]. Then, I'd yell to my teammates, 'Guess who's got me. Guess who's gonna get lit up tonight.' I'd even talk to the other coaches."

PHIL GAMBLE, CONNECTICUT: "Eric Murdock. He and [teammate] Tate George used to go at it. Eric would come up to me, and say, 'Your boy is scared.'"

BILLY GOODWIN, ST. JOHN'S: "Everyone on Georgetown. And it wasn't verbal; it was all body language. I remember the press conference after we beat them in the Garden [in Jan. 1983]. Patrick Ewing said, 'Every dog has its day. We'll see what happens when they come to our place.' We were like, 'Shit, we'll be there a day early!'"

MICHAEL GRAHAM, GEORGETOWN: "Pearl Washington used to say some off-the-wall stuff, and he would swing on you in a minute. He wasn't fearful of anyone. He even made Coach Thompson nervous. Coach would have nightmares about Pearl Washington."

OTIS HILL, SYRACUSE: "Danya Abrams. We're second cousins, and he knew there was nothing he could say about me that would bother me, so he'd always say things about my teammates. He got me so riled up."

EARL KELLEY, CONNECTICUT: "Me. Coach Calhoun and I had a falling out that lasted like 20 years. We played against him when he was coaching Northeastern. I'm doing my usual talking, and he says something to me like, 'Just play ball.' I said, 'Shut the fuck up, and put someone in the game who can stay in front of me.' He's an old-school, Irish dude, and pretty soon, he was controlling the entire state of Connecticut. I go to a lot of the games, and he would shake my hand, but you could tell he didn't want to talk to me. We finally reconciled like 10 years ago, when he called me into the locker room before a game, and started teasing me about it. He told me if there's anything he can do for me, to just let him know. He was genuine. Talking trash was just natural for me. I'd even mess with the guards we were recruiting. I'd tell them, 'No disrespect, but if you come here, I don't know where you're going to play. I play 40 minutes at the one and the two.' I told that to Mark Jackson when he visited."

JEROME LANE, PITTSBURGH: "Derrick Coleman used to talk some mess. He'd never shut up."

JASON LAWSON, VILLANOVA: "Probably Allen Iverson. I can still hear him saying, 'I'm about to give y'all 40! Can't nobody on y'all team stop me! They can't guard me, ref!' And [Iverson's teammate] Victor Page was just as bad. Our coach [Steve Lappas] begged us not to get involved in the trash-talking, but that was hard, being from Philly. I didn't mind punctuating a block with a 'Get that outta here!'"

JOHN LINEHAN, PROVIDENCE: "Not many people talked trash to me, because they knew I'd turn up the heat on them. I guess [Pittsburgh's] Vonteego Cummings and [Villanova's] John Celestand talked a little, but they paid for it."

FELIPE LOPEZ, ST. JOHN'S: "Khalid El-Amin talked some crazy junk, but he could back it up. He was one of the most deceiving guys I ever played against. He almost looked like he was out of shape, but he was the quickest guy on the court."

BOBBY MARTIN, PITTSBURGH: "[Syracuse's] Stevie Thompson and D.C. [Derrick Coleman] were neck and neck. They had a reason to talk trash, because they had a heck of a team. They'd yell across the court during warmups, 'We're gonna kick your asses today!' You knew you were in for a long day whenever you had to play them."

DWAYNE MCCLAIN, VILLANOVA: "The Georgetown players were aggressive and hardcore, but they didn't talk at all. [Boston College's] Dominic Pressley, Michael Adams's sidekick in the backcourt, talked more than anyone I've ever met. He was from D.C. We had a healthy rivalry, and wanted to kill each other every time we played. And Pearl Washington would walk over to the opposing bench, and say to the coach, 'Why are you putting this kid on me? You know he can't guard me.' I just thought he was being more factual than talking trash, though."

ROGER MCCREADY, BOSTON COLLEGE: "Earl Kelley would not shut up. You couldn't keep up with everything he was saying, so you just had to try to block it out. His voice was like a soundtrack to the game."

LANCE MILLER, VILLANOVA: "[Syracuse's] Adrian Autry talked a lot."

LAWRENCE MOTEN, SYRACUSE: "Jerry Walker talked every chance he got. And Donny Marshall—he was one of those slick, dirty players."

DAVID RUSSELL, ST. JOHN'S: "[Teammate] Kevin Williams used to scare the hell out of everyone on the floor, including us. One time in practice, he said to

George Garrison, 'When you touch that fucking ball, I'm gonna beat the shit out of you!' Patrick Ewing once swung an elbow at Kevin, and Kevin goes, 'You see all those guys over there at the end of my bench? We're all gonna beat your ass after the game.' Kevin was off the hook, man. Even Coach thought he was crazy."

CHRIS SMITH, CONNECTICUT: "Derrick Coleman and Sherman Douglas. Heck, pretty much everyone from Syracuse talked, probably because they had so much confidence. But D.C. used to catch alley-oops from Sherman, and he'd come down running his mouth."

JERRY WALKER, SETON HALL: "[Syracuse's] Conrad McRae, rest in peace, used to always get under my skin. We always had this love-hate thing since he was from New York, and I'm from Jersey. He was a slick talker."

JOHN WALLACE, SYRACUSE: "Me. I talked so much shit. I couldn't wait to jump ball at the beginning of a game. That's when I'd tell the other guy how much trouble he was in, how I'd make him my bitch. It got me going, because when you work yourself up into a frenzy like that, you better back it up."

DOUG WEST, VILLANOVA: "There were too many. Willie Glass from St. John's was one of them. I'll tell you who wasn't a trash-talker: Willie's teammate, Walter Berry. That guy would give you 30, and then laugh at you."

JEROME WILLIAMS, GEORGETOWN: "Donny Marshall. I recognize that he could play a little, but not as well as he thought. It's not like he was one of these elite players who could jump out of the gym."

WHAT DID YOU REALLY THINK OF
SYRACUSE'S 2-3 ZONE DEFENSE?

SCOTT BURRELL, CONNECTICUT: "The zone was good for what they recruited: big, long guys who could extend their arms and clog up the lane. A lot of teams were probably quicker than Syracuse, but the zone was perfect for their personnel."

STEVEN EDWARDS, MIAMI: "The heck with the zone. I couldn't deal with the cold weather. Coming from Miami, I hated road trips, because they were in some cold city in the Northeast. Nah, at least with the zone, you always knew what was coming. It was their signature. For shooters, it's great."

KERRY KITTLES, VILLANOVA: "It was weird, hard to describe. The Carrier Dome was this open arena with a basketball hoop sitting in the middle of what seemed like nowhere. Against the zone, you had to get into the seams, make jumpers, and try to find the easy shots around the rim. But that's easier said than done. The zone lured you into taking bad shots, and it had a way of dictating the tempo. It forced you into taking that tough, midrange shot, or driving into the middle where Conrad McRae or John Wallace was waiting for you. I thought we always played well against it, and that's a testament to our offensive will."

JOHN LINEHAN, PROVIDENCE: "My sophomore year in the dome, we made Syracuse come out of their zone. We jumped out to a 17-0 lead, and their students—who wouldn't sit down until they scored—were left standing for about nine minutes of game clock."

FELIPE LOPEZ, ST. JOHN'S: "It made you more of a catch-and-shoot player. You had to make quick decisions. That was what made the Big East so special— each team had its trademark like Syracuse's zone."

JERRY MCCULLOUGH, PITTSBURGH: "It made me a stationary guard. They'd put Adrian Autry and Lawrence Moten at the foul line, and they'd extend their arms out. There was no getting in the paint, so I'd just try to throw lobs over top of it."

MIKE MOSES, ST. JOHN'S: "It had the potential to expose a lot of individual deficiencies. We were often successful against Syracuse, but back then, there was no 3-point line. Every shot Chris [Mullin] made would've been a 3. Talk about a different scenario. With all those extra points, some of those games wouldn't even have been close. I'm sure Pearl Washington loved it. He never had to guard us, but we had to guard him."

JERRY WALKER, SETON HALL: "It was a work of art. Coach Boeheim really mastered the zone, and knew what type of player would fit it. His backcourt up top was always long, and could always give help down low. It was hard to crack. There weren't many soft spots."

**AS A HOYA, WERE YOU OFFENDED BY,
OR DID YOU EMBRACE THE LABEL OF THUG?**

FRED BROWN, GEORGETOWN: "I'm sure it was offensive to the university, but not to me. A prestigious school like that doesn't want to be characterized that way. Personally, I thought of it as a compliment. I just heard a politician on TV say, 'If they're talking about you, you must be doing something right.' That's how I looked at it. I can tell you that I wasn't reading the press clippings about us. I didn't pay attention to any of it. I was busy trying to get an education. But I will say this: We didn't start anything, but if another team did, we sure finished it."

JOEY BROWN, GEORGETOWN: "It was offensive to me and especially to Coach Thompson. Not many people understand the true meaning of Hoya Paranoia. Most people thought it stood for the way Georgetown intimidated opponents in the '80s, or how Coach thought the media picked on him and his players. But it really was about Coach Thompson being scared for his players, and trying to protect them as best as he could. He really was paranoid, and he had a right to be. Patrick Ewing used to get death threats and letters filled with racial epithets, but he and a lot of the media didn't know it, because Coach shielded everyone from that. He was a father figure. Let's say Georgetown was playing Villanova at the Spectrum [in Philadelphia]. Coach would have the team staying at a hotel 20 miles outside the city, because he didn't want anyone to know where they were staying. He didn't want them to be a target. I'm the only one in my family to graduate from college, and I wouldn't have done it if it wasn't for Coach. I'll be forever grateful for him."

ROBERT CHURCHWELL, GEORGETOWN: "We embraced it. That persona was formed well before I got there. Coach Thompson was brilliant in forming that us-against-the-world mentality. He recruited tough, physical guys who wanted to be a part of that and could live up to that standard. We played some hard-ass, hell-a-fied defense! That's why so many blacks loved Georgetown, because Coach stood up for what he believed in. He was no nonsense, no bullshit, and it was love him or leave him."

MICHAEL GRAHAM, GEORGETOWN: "It was sort of offensive, being an all-black team at an all-white institution. I mean, we had a lot more to offer than just playing basketball. I guess I had a lot to do with that [violent] perception people had of us. Yeah, we played rough, but we weren't out to hurt anyone. I just let my frustrations and the difficulty I had adjusting to Coach Thompson out on the court. One night against Providence, I think I scored the first 12 points of the game, and he took me out, and I never got back in."

JAREN JACKSON, GEORGETOWN: "Neither. It didn't affect me. I heard all the rumblings about how we played and what our reputation was. Was it motivation for some players? Perhaps. But I didn't need anybody to call me a name to motivate me. I had motivation enough in practice. Coach Thompson did a great job of closing the doors, and making sure the way you played in practice was how you played in a game."

JEROME WILLIAMS, GEORGETOWN: "Man, we loved it. We were bona-fide thugs. We walked on the court with a whole body armor of thuggery. You didn't want to play us. Our opponents were thankful for the guys in the stripes, because they were there to keep the peace. Coach Thompson turned us against each other in practice, so when it was game time, we were happily ready to take the abuse out on someone else. We oozed confidence. And with a warrior like Allen Iverson on our side, we didn't think anyone could beat us. We'd be shocked when other teams were actually in the game."

> ## BESIDES YOUR OWN, WHAT COACH IN THE CONFERENCE WOULD YOU HAVE MOST LIKED TO PLAY FOR?

RAFAEL ADDISON, SYRACUSE: "Rollie Massimino. I always had a good relationship with him. He seemed to be a blue-collar guy like me."

MARQUES BRAGG, PROVIDENCE: "John Thompson. I always thought I was a Hoya. I modeled my game after the way Georgetown played. They were strong and physical, and that's the way I played. I would've been a perfect fit there, but I was a late bloomer, and they didn't recruit me."

SCOTT BURRELL, CONNECTICUT: "If I wanted to play offense, Jim Boeheim. If I wanted to play defense, John Thompson."

BILL CURLEY, BOSTON COLLEGE: "Jim Calhoun. He had a great vision and passion for the game. I'm not surprised he went on to win three national titles."

OTIS HILL, SYRACUSE: "No one. Coach Boeheim was so much fun to play for. People have no clue how funny that guy is. His sense of humor was great. One time at West Virginia, we were getting killed at halftime. He comes in the locker room, fuming, not knowing what to say or where to even begin. He looks at the first two guys he sees—I think it was Jason Cipolla and Marius Janulis—and unloads on them. Coach said, 'You two fucking guys! You two pieces of shit! You should flush yourselves down the toilet!' The whole team started cracking up, and even Coach started laughing. We went out in the second half, and lost even worse. He ran us like crazy the whole week after that."

FELIPE LOPEZ, ST. JOHN'S: "John Thompson. ESPN held a conference for racial issues in sports, and we were both on the panel. Just to hear him speak and have him take me under his wing—I felt how much he cared for minorities, not just as players and professionals, but as humans. Plus, I have respect for him giving Allen Iverson an opportunity when no one else would give him a chance."

ROGER MCCREADY, BOSTON COLLEGE: "Either Lou Carnesecca or P.J. Carlesimo. They were both great communicators, and brought out the best in their players. They could be playful in the heat of competition, too. During a game, they'd say things like, 'Cut it out! You're killing us today!'"

JERRY MCCULLOUGH, PITTSBURGH: "John Thompson. The vibe on his bench was different than anything I'd ever seen. The enthusiasm his players had, man, was incredible. They'd echo everything he said: 'Shooter, shooter! Cutter, cutter!' And they had this clap that was contagious."

LANCE MILLER, VILLANOVA: "John Thompson. Growing up, we used to love Georgetown. We'd all buy the Nikes with 'Hoyas' written on the back. Heck, I'll admit it: I rooted for Georgetown in 1985 when they lost to 'Nova."

LAWRENCE MOTEN, SYRACUSE: "Anyone but John Thompson. Nothing personal against him. We went to the same high school [Archbishop Carroll], and he even coached there early in his career, so we're alumni brothers. But his style of play didn't fit mine. I liked to get up and down the floor. If you weren't a big man in his system, he wasn't trying to hear what you had to say."

JAY MURPHY, BOSTON COLLEGE: "Lou Carnesecca. I loved the freedom his players had. He let them play."

CHRIS SMITH, CONNECTICUT: "John Thompson. I had a lot of admiration for his militaristic approach. He had his guys wearing suits and ties and wouldn't let them talk to the media. It was never about the individual; it was always about the team."

JERRY WALKER, SETON HALL: "Lou Carnesecca. He had a lot of passion and a great personality. He was one of the forefathers of the Big East. I was close to going to St. John's, but in the end, I couldn't go to a New York school."

JOHN WALLACE, SYRACUSE: "Rick Barnes. He and [assistant coach] Fran Fraschilla were great recruiters. They sold me and my mom on getting away from home and making a name for myself. If I could've signed as a sophomore in high school, I would've gone to Providence."

ROBERT WERDANN, ST. JOHN'S: "I couldn't imagine playing for anyone other than Coach Carnesecca. And I wasn't mature enough as a college student to really appreciate him, like I should've. He wrapped his arms around you. Even if you resisted, he still tried. The lessons I learned from him I still use to this day. He taught you responsibility. He basically taught you a new language. You had the

English language, and you had the Louie language. And the Louie language was a bit more colorful, if you know what I mean."

JEROME WILLIAMS, GEORGETOWN: "Jim Boeheim. Syracuse has a history of coming down and grabbing guys from D.C. and Baltimore. If he would've come for me, I probably would've signed. And I've told him that before."

WHO WAS YOUR TEAM'S X-FACTOR, THE PLAYER YOU THOUGHT NEVER GOT THE CREDIT HE DESERVED, EVEN THOUGH HIS CONTRIBUTIONS WERE CRITICAL TO YOUR SUCCESS?

TERRY DEHERE, SETON HALL: "Gordon Winchester. He was our glue guy, our best wing defender. Gordon always had to guard the other team's best scorer."

EARL KELLEY, CONNECTICUT: "Norman Bailey. If the other team went box-and-one on me, he was the other guy who could go out and get us 20. I thought we could've made the tournament my freshman year, but he was academically ineligible toward the end of the season. Without him, we had no chance."

KERRY KITTLES, VILLANOVA: "Jonathan Haynes. He never got any accolades, but he was the meat and soul of our team. There wasn't a tougher player I ever played with than Jon, and I played with Kenyon Martin. Trust me, you want Jon in your foxhole."

FELIPE LOPEZ, ST. JOHN'S: "Charles Minlend and Rowan Barrett. [A 6-6, 225-pound power forward] Charles was undersized, but he was a warrior. And Rowan did a bit of everything for us."

DICKEY SIMPKINS, PROVIDENCE: "Abdul Abdullah. He was the maestro of our offense, and kept everyone happy. Rob Phelps was another unsung hero. He could've been a prolific scorer, but he sacrificed a lot for the sake of chemistry."

CHRIS SMITH, CONNECTICUT: "Nadav Henefeld. He was the engine of our defense. [Henefeld averaged 3.7 steals per game to become the Big East Rookie of the Year in 1989-90, his lone season in college.] It didn't take him long to adjust to the American game. He fit in right away."

JOHN WALLACE, SYRACUSE: "Lazarus Sims. He was the best passer in college basketball that year [1995-96], and got everyone the ball at perfect times."

WHAT'S ONE INSTANCE IN YOUR COLLEGE CAREER—GOOD OR BAD, ON THE COURT OR OFF—THAT YOU'LL NEVER FORGET?

ABDUL ABDULLAH, PROVIDENCE: "The semifinals of the Big East Tournament against UConn my senior year. I remember being in the elevator at our hotel, and people saw our warmup gear and asked us who we were playing. UConn was the No. 2 team in the nation, and people were like, 'Too bad. You're gonna get smacked.' In our locker room before the game, we could hear Donny Marshall through the wall, getting his team hyped up. He was barking, 'Let's go, big dogs!' I looked at Dickey [Simpkins], and he was just shaking his head. He said, 'Well, it's time to stick it up their asses!' While we were warming up on the floor, they did a flashback to 1984 on the big screen. It was the 10-year anniversary of the final between Syracuse and Georgetown. They showed highlights of Pearl Washington shaking Michael Jackson to pieces, and cutting up Georgetown's press. Pearl was my inspiration growing up, and I got chills seeing that again. I knew there was no way we were going to lose that game."

DANYA ABRAMS, BOSTON COLLEGE: "When we upset [North] Carolina, that made it clear that I'd made the right decision to go to B.C. As the only freshman in a starting lineup with guys like Bill Curley, Howard Eisley, and Malcolm Huckaby, I got my butt kicked all year that season. But those guys gave me confidence, and when we beat Carolina, that set the tone for the rest of my college career. I mean, just months before that, I was sitting on my couch watching them win the national championship and thinking nobody can beat these guys."

DONNY BROWN, PROVIDENCE: "For me, it was the relationships. Coming out of L.A., I didn't know the differences among Italians, Irish, Jews. But when I went to Providence, people from each of those cultures embraced me, and it had a big impact on my life. Rhode Island is a great state, and that's why I spent 30 years of my life there. It taught me a lot about people."

FRED BROWN, GEORGETOWN: "I'd say the lessons I learned about people in general, society. Seeing the reaction people had when we lost [in the national championship] by a point, then seeing the reaction when we won. The difference was fascinating to me. The response between winning that game and losing that game was like night and day. We got to the final and lost by a point to Michael

Jordan and James Worthy. I think that's a hell of an accomplishment. Yeah, we lost the game, but we're not losers. We just fell short of the goal. But that's not what everyone else thinks. I get that it's important for the administration, in terms of dollars and cents, and for the alumni who want bragging rights. But let's be honest. We won it two years later with basically the same team. We scored a few more points than the other team, and all of a sudden, the world thinks we're the greatest thing since ice cream. But we weren't any better than we were two years before. People hang their hats on winning too much."

JOEY BROWN, GEORGETOWN: "This one practice, after we get dressed and walk on to the floor, Coach Thompson tells us to get on the line. I thought that was a little strange, since we did our sprints at the end of practice. So he blew the whistle, and we ran up and back probably about 10 times. Then, Coach let us get a drink out of our water bottles. As I'm drinking my water, guys are looking at each other with this puzzled look on their faces. I'm thinking, 'What the hell is going on?' Coach said to me, 'Joey, how's your water taste?' I told him it tasted fine. Then, he looked at Church [Robert Churchwell], and asked him the same question. And Church said the water was all right. Then, he asked John Jacques and Kevin Millen how theirs tasted. They said, 'Now that you mentioned it, it tastes kind of funny.' Knowing that Lamont Morgan was a big partier, Coach goes to Lamont, 'Take a sip of John's and Kevin's water.' So he takes a swig, and is like, 'Damn, Coach, that's beer!' Coach had found out that John and Kevin were out the whole night before, drinking at some concert. He said, 'You're damn right it is! And it ain't that cheap shit you college kids like! That's Heineken. And we're all standing here until John and Kevin drink their whole bottles.' We were dying, laughing. They had to drink like 25 ounces of beer, then suffer through practice."

BRYAN CAVER, SETON HALL: "My sophomore year against Georgetown at the Meadowlands, when I went coast to coast and laid it in at the buzzer. Robert Churchwell had just hit a 3 to tie it with 5.5 seconds left in overtime. We called timeout, and P.J. [Carlesimo] said, 'Get as close as you can, draw a foul, and go to the line.' I told whoever was in-bounding it, to give it to me on the move. I knew I'd have space, since we were in the bonus, and they wouldn't want to foul. Alonzo Mourning had fouled out earlier, and they didn't have anyone to protect the rim. So I got the ball with a full head of steam, and when I got to half-court, I kind of glanced up at the shot clock. I didn't think I'd get that far that quick, so I kept going. As soon as I released the ball, I could hear the horn. Our fans stormed the court. It was a great moment for me. After the game, P.J. told reporters that I didn't do what he wanted me to do. I'm like, 'Damn, Coach!' What the hell is that?"

74

BILL CURLEY, BOSTON COLLEGE: "The win over Carolina showed me how crazy, how unique sports can be. We just came off a beat-down from Georgetown in the quarterfinals of the Big East Tournament. I fouled out with 16 minutes left in the game, and the next few days were so negative. Even on Selection Sunday, nobody wanted to be there. It was an incredible situation. Everyone was waiting for Coach [Jim] O'Brien to get fired, guys were fighting in practice, and the media was criticizing our senior class. There was just a cloud of negativity hovering over our team. When we got away for the tournament, though, things somehow came together. Coach concocted a hell of a plan against Carolina, and we followed it to a T. After the win, all of a sudden, the seniors were the greatest class in the history of the program."

ERIC EBERZ, VILLANOVA: "The Old Dominion loss—that's the only thing people want to talk about. I'm like, 'Hey, we won the NIT, the Big East Tournament, and more than 20 games almost every year.' But that's all they want to remember."

PHIL GAMBLE, CONNECTICUT: "Going from the bottom of the barrel to winning the NIT my junior year. I'll never forget losing to Villanova on a last-second shot in Coach Calhoun's first year. After the game, Rollie [Massimino] made a snotty comment to Coach, something like, 'You almost had it. Maybe next time.' Coach went berserk, and tried to go after him. [Assistant coaches] Howie Dickenman and Dave Leitao had to hold him back. Rollie goes, 'Ah, shut up!' When Coach came in the locker room, he was fuming. He started screaming, 'We'll never be 9-19 again! Never again!' He was right, because they haven't. Going from that to NIT champions was special. Coach Calhoun had us in the best shape of our lives. Cliff [Robinson] got into foul trouble against Ohio State in the final, and he told me I had to step up. I hit five 3-pointers, and we won by five points. We listened to Coach, dedicated ourselves to him, and all the hard work paid off like he said it would. When we got back to campus that night, there were parties everywhere. There was this spot we called The Jungle, it was a circular area in the middle of all the dorms. Students were dragging furniture and couches out there, and lighting them on fire. Winning the NIT was a big deal, because they hadn't won anything before. When my playing career ended, I sunk into a deep depression. I wasn't ready for it to be over. Mentally, I kept coming back to moments like that. It was hard for me to adjust when all the cheering and clapping stopped. I withdrew from everyone. It took years for me to get out of the funk."

BILLY GOODWIN, ST. JOHN'S: "My entire senior year [1982-83]. We beat [defending national champion] North Carolina to start the season in the Hall of

Fame game in Springfield [Mass.], and ran off like 14 wins in a row. Then, we had a chance to win the [Big East] regular season against Villanova at the Spectrum. The game was tied with seven seconds left with Chris [Mullin] at the foul line. Of course, he hits the first. And this was back before they had the 3-point line, so we figured at the very least, they could take us to overtime. But Chris misses the second! Are you kidding me? I think he hadn't missed a free throw in like 10 games before that. We found out after the game that the foul shot would've been his 1,000th point. Well, we must have been paralyzed with shock, because they get the rebound, push it ahead, and [Villanova center] John Pinone nails a fade-away at the buzzer to win it for them. So we had to enter the first Big East Tournament at the Garden as the third seed. We play Pitt in the first round, and this whole tournament is a perfect example of how Coach [Carnesecca] used to be. Before the game, he tells us, 'The media wants to make this into some big thing. Don't listen to their bullshit. It's just a game like any other. Go out there and play like you always do, and let the chips fall where they may.' So we're loose, and win by double digits. The next game, we're down to Villanova by 12 at the half. Coach comes in [the locker room] screaming, 'You fucking guys! Your friends, your parents, the whole student body is here, and you're blowing it! What the hell is wrong with you?' We went on a huge run, and outscored them by more than 20 points in the second half. Before the final against Boston College, Coach said, 'Well, we can't lose now. Not in our backyard.' We just rode the wave of 19,000 people in the Garden. We won by eight, and the game had been over for 20 minutes, and the place was still rocking. Fans running around everywhere. Journalists and photographers grabbing at us. That week, I was on the cover of *Sports Illustrated*, sitting on the rim with the net hanging around my neck. Coach told us after the game, 'Guys, it's not that you won it. It's that you won it here.'"

MICHAEL GRAHAM, GEORGETOWN: "During the Final Four in Seattle, I was bawling just about every other day. We were the top seed in the West [Region], and had already spent like two weeks out there. I'd never been away from home that long. I didn't want to lose, but I was ready to come home. I missed my mom too much. I took all my emotions out on the floor. In warmups against Houston [in the national championship], all the guys from Houston, except Akeem, were looking over at me, smirking and whispering to each other, instead of concentrating on what they were doing. I sensed we were gonna win. I told my teammates in the huddle, 'We got 'em. They're too worried about me.' Akeem was the quickest big man I ever played against. He was ready to be a star, but we got the job done. After winning the championship, I lost my urgency. My mom died of a brain hemorrhage at 42, so I had to take care of my two younger brothers. My priorities changed, and I left the program."

OTIS HILL, SYRACUSE: "The NCAA Tournament my junior year, and getting to the national championship game. Our matchup against [top-seeded] Kansas [led by Paul Pierce and Jacque Vaughn] in the Elite Eight was personal. There was an article in the paper the day before the game, and I guess Raef LaFrentz was asked about me. He said, 'We're not worried about Otis Hill. We just have to stop John Wallace.' Then Scot Pollard chimed in, and said, 'Once we take care of Wallace, we'll be in good position.' [Syracuse assistant coach] Wayne Morgan put an enlarged photocopy of the story in my locker before practice. I practiced that day so angry, and it carried over to the game. Some people thought I talked to myself during games, but I was actually talking to my father. He died of a heart attack in '94, and talking to him helped me keep our relationship alive. Early on against Kansas, I got the ball down low, and did an up-and-under and dunked on LaFrentz and Pollard. I never talked trash, but when I came down the court, I was screaming, 'It's gonna be a long fucking day!' Roy Williams came up to me after we won, and said, 'Son, you played a hell of a game.' Then, we played Mississippi State in the Final Four. Derrick Coleman was there, and he said to me beforehand, 'I don't know, O. Erick Dampier is a big dude. I think you might be in trouble.' I said to myself, 'Here we go again. I'm gonna have to prove myself again.' I scored a couple baskets early, and they started doubling me. I'm thinking, 'They're leaving John open? This is great. We're gonna win by 20!' We hung tough in the final against Kentucky, but they had six guys who [later] played in the NBA. The whole thing was just an amazing ride."

MALCOLM HUCKABY, BOSTON COLLEGE: "I had grown up dreaming of playing in the Garden. My freshman year, we were getting ready to board a plane or a bus—I can't remember what it was—to go to my first Big East Tournament. That's when all of our assistant coaches came in the locker room with tears in their eyes. They told us that Coach O'Brien's wife passed away. [Christine O'Brien died suddenly of heart failure at 41.] Coach and his wife had two teenage daughters, and to this day, I can still see Mrs. O'Brien's face at our games. It was a sad time for the program, and needless to say, it wasn't the trip to the Garden I had envisioned."

JAREN JACKSON, GEORGETOWN: "My senior year, Coach Thompson was able to schedule a game against LSU at the [Louisiana] Superdome, since we had so many guys from New Orleans. He gave us a chance to play in front of family and friends for the first time in college. We lost [82-80], and Chris Jackson went off as usual. It was nationally televised and set the record for the largest crowd to ever see a regular-season game in the history of college basketball. I scored 26 points, and caught a nice alley-oop. But what made it so special is that my father was there.

Growing up, he worked a lot, and I had a lot of siblings, so he had a lot of other priorities. He never attended many of my games, but I didn't hold it against him. He wasn't really a fan of basketball, but he was a fan of me. At halftime, I could hear his voice calling my name. I looked up, and pointed at him. That was a big moment for me."

EARL KELLEY, CONNECTICUT: "My junior year, we beat Syracuse at the Carrier Dome [70-68 in front of 30,136 fans] when they were ranked seventh in the nation. We were up most of the second half by one point or three points, an odd number. This was before the 3-point line, and we kept trading baskets. Well, we eventually fell behind late. But I scored 12 of our final 14 points, including six straight free throws with less than 30 seconds left. I hit both the front and back ends of three straight one-and-ones with fans screaming at me, calling me a traitor for reneging on my commitment there. Everyone knew I was gonna get the ball, but they couldn't stop me. Boeheim was so pissed. The last two foul shots—I'll never forget. I stepped to the line and motioned for the crowd to make more noise. The cameraman was on the baseline under the basket. I took three dribbles, spun the ball, and looked right in the heart of the camera. I said, 'It's all over, folks!' Swish. Nothing but net. I did the same thing on the second shot, too. After the game, a UPI [United Press International] reporter asked me what I said to the camera. I told him, and the next day, he wrote that I had ice water in my veins."

KERRY KITTLES, VILLANOVA: "My junior year, when I ended up winning Big East Player of the Year. We beat Syracuse [89-87 in overtime] at the Spectrum [in mid-February]. Lawrence Moten absolutely lit me up. [Moten scored 36 points, shooting 15-for-27 from the field.] After the game, [teammates] Alvin Williams and Jon Haynes gave me so much crap about it. They were like, 'Dude, he torched you.' And they were right. They never let me hear the end of it. Then, Jim Boeheim said something to the media about how Lawrence should be Player of the Year. Maybe I heard it, maybe I didn't. I told my team, 'Whoever we play next is gonna get it.' Just so happened that we were playing at UConn four days later, and they were the No. 1 team in the country. We went up there, and won by 23. [*The Philadelphia Inquirer* said that the 'game started as an upset and evolved into an ambush.'] I had 37 points, and 25 were in the first half."

JEROME LANE, PITTSBURGH: "Shattering the backboard. Here's what I remember, like it was yesterday: It didn't matter where you were on the fast break, [point guard] Sean Miller was gonna find you. And any time I was near the basket, I was dunking it. This time was no different. I just didn't expect the rim to come down with me. In the locker room [while officials were setting up a new basket], guys were picking glass out of their hair. It didn't hit me until we came back out to resume the game, and the fans gave us a two-minute standing ovation. They wouldn't stop cheering. When the game started back up, I tried to do it again, but the backboard didn't move. I guess I busted up the fake one, so they figured they'd better put up a real one! Seriously, though. That moment brought me a lot of fame, but it solidified in people's minds that all I could do is dunk. I had other skills—I could rebound, I could handle the ball, I could do a lot of things. But people didn't pay attention to it."

JASON LAWSON, VILLANOVA: "Losing to Old Dominion. I felt personally responsible, because I fouled a 3-point shooter in the corner when we were up by three at the end of regulation. Dude [Petey Sessoms] hit all three free throws to tie it up. I remember coming home that summer, and guys were like, 'Damn, I lost money on y'all.' And every now and then, my teammates and I will get together, and they'll say, 'You know, Jay, if you wouldn't have fouled him, we would've won.' I'm like, 'Man, tell me how you really feel.' It was tough, because we had a good team and a good draw in the bracket. It's not that we overlooked Old Dominion. They just made a lot of tough shots down the stretch."

BOBBY MARTIN, PITTSBURGH: "Early in my sophomore season, I was having a good game against Seton Hall and Anthony Avent on CBS. My academic advisor whispered to me toward the end of the game, and said, 'When you get interviewed, the announcer is going to say the new Bobby Martin has arrived. Tell him no. The real Bobby Martin has arrived.' And that's what I did. Charles Smith was gone, and I was no longer in his shadow. That's when I could finally start to showcase everything I could do."

JASON MATTHEWS, PITTSBURGH: "Winning the Big East [regular season] as a freshman at Syracuse was extra sweet, since they had Earl Duncan, my high school teammate, and Stevie Thompson [another L.A. native]. Stevie was a phenomenal defender, but he mastered the art of nicking your elbow just enough when you were shooting, so you had to alter your shot. And the refs never called it. I'd argue with the refs and say, 'How am I almost leading the Big East in field-goal percentage, but I come here and throw up bricks off the side of the backboard?' Of course, I'll always remember standing underneath the basket when [teammate] Jerome Lane shattered the glass."

DWAYNE MCCLAIN, VILLANOVA: "As if you had to ask. One hundred years from now, I think they'll still be talking about our upset of Georgetown, because you'll never see a team shoot 80 percent from the floor over the course of a game.

[The Wildcats shot 78.6 percent.] We didn't end the season with a lot of momentum, so when we were selected for the tournament, we said all bets are off. Now, we're playing with house money. For the seniors—me, Gary McLain, and Ed Pinckney—we'd been to the Elite Eight twice, and we wanted to make good on our promise to Coach Mass and win a national championship. Knowing it was our last go-round, our practice sessions were longer, and we didn't want to leave. We paid more attention to detail, and put our nose to the grind. The next thing you know, you look up, and you're in the Final Four. We were happy to have Memphis State [in the national semifinals]. I'll admit: It was a blessing to not have to play St. John's again. When we won and got to the finals against Georgetown, their scare tactics didn't work against us, because we were familiar with them. It's not what Georgetown didn't do that day. It's what we did. To this day, Patrick Ewing is reluctant to give us credit [for our win]. That's the warrior in him. He may not want to talk about it, but he has to recognize it."

DARREN MORNINGSTAR, PITTSBURGH: "Early in my senior year, we won at [No. 4] Kentucky [85-67] in the second round of the preseason NIT when were 20-point underdogs. I had 27 points and 10 rebounds. That was my signature game. Dick Vitale was on the mic, and we snapped their 22-game winning streak at Rupp Arena. I also remember a lot of the dumb shit I did, like growing sideburns so people would notice me. Hey, I thought it was a good shtick."

MIKE MOSES, ST. JOHN'S: "The NCAA Tournament my senior year. We had expectations beyond anything I could have ever imagined. I think 29 of our 35 games were on national television. In 1985! We had to go to Denver for the Sweet 16 and Elite Eight, and I remember Chris [Mullin] gathering all the seniors when we got there. Together, we went to everyone's hotel room, and made them unpack and put their clothes in the drawers. We said, 'We're gonna be here for a while, so let's settle in and get comfortable.' That was a lot of fun, hanging out in the mountains after the games. We were there over St. Patrick's Day, and with Chris being Irish, let's just say we had fun. I remember all of our game plans in the tournament, what we were going to do to contain Joe Kleine [Arkansas], Kenny 'Sky' Walker [Kentucky], then Spud Webb [N.C. State]. When we got to the Final Four, I tried to enjoy the moment, but there were so many distractions. The media would ask you the stupidest stuff, because they had a paper to fill with stories mostly about nothing. We were happy when Saturday came. I certainly wish we could've played Memphis State, but it didn't work out that way."

LAWRENCE MOTEN, SYRACUSE: "I was a freshman, and it was our third or fourth game of the season. We were playing Florida State in the Big East/ACC

Challenge at The Omni in Atlanta. A couple days before that, Michael Edwards, one of our guards, went down with an ankle injury. So we enter the locker room, and Coach Boeheim had the starters written on the board, like always, and who they were checking. I saw my name next to Adrian Autry's in our backcourt, and couldn't believe it. After Coach talked to us, part of his routine was to give us five to ten minutes to be by ourselves. Some guys would meditate; some guys would go stretch in the tunnel. I went in search of a pay phone, so I could call my mother. I finally found one, dialed the seven digits, and she picked up. I said, 'Mom, I got a starting spot tonight!' She screamed so loud, and her words after that, I'll never forget. She said, 'Baby, don't ever give it back!' It was a thrilling moment for me. We won the game, I played well on TV, and I went on to have a great career."

JAY MURPHY, BOSTON COLLEGE: "The tournaments were so memorable. I played four years in the NBA and seven more in Europe, and let me tell you, there's nothing like the Big East Tournament and the NCAA Tournament. They were just so pure. When the Big East Tournament moved to the Garden [in 1983], we made it to the finals against St. John's. And the year before that, we made the Elite Eight as an eight seed. We knocked off [top-seeded] DePaul and Terry Cummings, then lost to Houston's Phi Slama Jama. I swear that region was one of the toughest in the history of the tournament."

JOHN PINONE, VILLANOVA: "Definitely my buzzer-beater against St. John's. In the postgame press conference, when Coach Carnesecca was done speaking with reporters, he handed me the microphone, and said, 'Enjoy this, John. This one you'll remember for a lifetime.' He was right: I have. That game was at home, but I also loved winning on the road. I think we might have been one of the first teams to beat Syracuse in the Carrier Dome. There were 30,000 fans there, and you could hear a pin drop. There was nothing better than stealing one on the road. All the fans go home quiet."

CONSTANTIN POPA, MIAMI: "For me, it was all four years, the whole experience, because Coach [Leonard] Hamilton worked very hard to get in touch with me. I knew very little about American basketball, except Michael Jordan, Magic Johnson, and Larry Bird. And I knew almost nothing about college basketball. I was living in Bucharest, and with communism and all that, there was very little connection to the Western World. I don't know how Coach Ham found me, but he did."

DAVID RUSSELL, ST. JOHN'S: "Winning the MVP of the Holiday Festival as a freshman. We beat Boston College in the final. I came off the bench and had like six dunks. [Teammate and All-American] Reggie Carter, who ended up being drafted by the Knicks, said, 'How the hell does a rookie win that award?' No one on the team could believe it."

RONY SEIKALY, SYRACUSE: "It wasn't just the national championship game my junior year. It was the journey to get there, the five games before that. Up until that season, Coach Boeheim had never won a second game in the NCAA Tournament, so the talk around Syracuse was always two-and-out, two-and-out. Once we got over that hump and won that second game, it didn't matter that we had to play Florida or [North] Carolina. We felt like the heavy lifting had already been done. College basketball was like a honeymoon for me. It was the sport in its purest form. You played for the name on the front of your jersey, not on the back like in the pros. Even though in the pros you're still a team, you do what you've got to do to get paid, to take care of your family. In college, if your coach tells you that all he wants you to do is set picks, you do it. In the NBA, guys won't do that, because at the end of the year when their contract is up, they're not gonna get another one [based on their ability to set picks]."

DICKEY SIMPKINS, PROVIDENCE: "My senior year, we were 12-9 and ran off eight straight to win the Big East Tournament. What fueled that streak was a regular-season game at home against Georgetown. It was originally scheduled to be on CBS, but there was a little bit of snow, so Coach Thompson wouldn't let his team make the trip. That made us so mad, because they stood us up when we had that rare opportunity to play on CBS. We beat them in the rescheduled game, then in the Big East championship. We had a chip on our shoulder that whole week in New York. We stayed at the Marriott Marquis, and there were swarms of people around, all underestimating us. Each win created more speculation that Coach Barnes was gonna leave, and it caused a little tension within the team. Austin Croshere was just a freshman then, and he was thinking about transferring. I called a team meeting and told the guys, 'Look, Coach is gonna do what's best for his family. He's gonna make the best decision for the business he's in. Whatever you all decide you want to do after the season is up to you. But whatever you choose, winning is gonna help you either way. If we win, a more-attractive coach is gonna want to come here. If you want to transfer, schools are gonna want a winner.' We went out, and got the job done. It was the program's first Big East Tournament title."

CHRIS SMITH, CONNECTICUT: "Playing against Providence. [Teammate] Tate George and Eric Murdock hated each other, I guess since they were both from Jersey. So that made games with Providence especially interesting."

ROBERT WERDANN, ST. JOHN'S: "The progression we made during my four years is what I'll always remember the most. Coach used to tell us, 'You're in the window at Macy's. You're on display, and have every opportunity to own this city.' He was absolutely right. We won the NIT my freshman year, and not to downplay it, but it was a stepping stone. We knew where we wanted to go. We got to the second round of the NCAAs my sophomore year, and advanced to the Elite Eight my junior year. Unfortunately, I got injured as a senior, and the wheels fell off. But that doesn't put a cloud over my experience. To see us come together as a unit, as a group of young men, under the tutelage of some great people—like Lou Carnesecca, Brian Mahoney, and Ron Rutledge—that was what the ride was all about."

DOUG WEST, VILLANOVA: "Mine was before my career even started. I had already signed with Villanova, and had attended their last regular-season game my senior year of high school. Pitt beat them by like 20-something points. It was a straight beat-down. At that time, no one thought they would get in the field of 64, let alone win a championship. Fast-forward a month, the night they won it, I was in a hotel in Pittsburgh with all the other [All-Star] players for the Dapper Dan [Roundball Classic]. Everyone wanted Georgetown to win. Back then, the Georgetown Nike gear and sneakers were so popular. When Villanova did it, man, what a feeling it was."

> MOST PEOPLE POINT TO BOSTON COLLEGE'S DEFECTION FROM THE
> CONFERENCE IN 2005 AS THE BEGINNING OF THE END FOR THE
> BIG EAST, AND SYRACUSE'S DEPARTURE IN 2013 AS THE FINAL NAIL
> IN ITS COFFIN. AT ANY RATE, DESCRIBE YOUR EMOTIONS WHEN
> IT BECAME APPARENT THAT THE BIG EAST IN ITS PROPER FORM
> WOULD CEASE TO EXIST.

RAFAEL ADDISON, SYRACUSE: "It made me look back and come to the realization that I was in paradise. We couldn't enjoy it then, because if you stopped to smell the roses, someone was taking your place. But now, I can say, 'I did it. I was there. I was a part of it.' The Big East will never be the same. Man, college basketball hasn't been the same. The D-League is what the Big East used to be, because all those players stayed in college. Now, all you can do is reminisce, because you can't get it back. When you see the guys [you played with and against], all you can do is hug them, thank them, laugh with them, cry with them. Then, you've got to move on."

MARQUES BRAGG, PROVIDENCE: "I never understood the dynamics between football and basketball schools, but I'll tell you that it felt good knowing that I was a part of history that can never be duplicated. You'll never see a conference like the original Big East ever again."

SCOTT BURRELL, CONNECTICUT: "The name Big East should never be used again. It's embarrassing. No disrespect to those other teams, but you can't have schools in the middle of the country calling themselves the Big East."

ROBERT CHURCHWELL, GEORGETOWN: "As I get older, I get more into history and the past, and being a part of something that made sports history like that was such a blessing. Being a part of those battles and seeing the conference die like that—a piece of you kind of died with it. There will never be another event like the Big East Tournament. It never failed to live up to the hype. In some respects, it was often better than the NCAA Tournament."

BILL CURLEY, BOSTON COLLEGE: "I thought of Media Day in New York City and the nice hotels, and all the luncheons that kicked off the Big East Tournament. You'd share a meal with the other teams. Everyone was civil, but there was no question we wanted to kill each other. The conference just won't ever be the same."

TERRY DEHERE, SETON HALL: "Pure sadness. As a kid growing up in the metropolitan area, you'd live for those Saturday Big East games. You'd run to the TV set, so you wouldn't miss the game. That's been gone for a long time, though."

ERIC EBERZ, VILLANOVA: "It's a shame there will never be another conference like the Big East again. When I heard Syracuse was leaving for the ACC, it wasn't just sad; it was weird. It made no sense to me. I guess it's a tale of the times with football and the money involved. The other day, I was talking to some Villanova people, and they were telling me about flying to Nebraska to play Creighton, and the game being on at 10 PM on the East Coast. When I played, it was mostly bus trips to major cities. Now it's plane rides to the Midwest."

OTIS HILL, SYRACUSE: "A lot of people have asked me that question, and I've always tried to give the politically correct answer. But now, I'll speak from the heart. I truly hated to see something so special dismantled like that. It hurt. Still does."

BOBBY MARTIN, PITTSBURGH: "It made me sick. It forced me to take inventory of what's really going on. This isn't about education. And you know what? That's cool. I'm a capitalist at heart. God Bless America! But let's stop the charade. Stop trying to pretend that it isn't about money. Because that's all it is."

JASON MATTHEWS, PITTSBURGH: "I immediately thought of Dave Gavitt and his legacy. I want people to really understand who he was. He knew our parents by their first names, was always asking about your grades, and making sure you were on track to get your degree. He did so much for me. He was involved with USA Basketball, and even though he never said anything to me, I know he nominated me for the national team I played on [at the FIBA Americas Championship in Mexico City in 1989]. And I'm sure it took a little prodding to convince others that I belonged, because I was the only guy on that team who never signed an NBA contract. We were stacked—we had Billy Owens, Lionel Simmons, Gary Payton, Chris Corchiani, Matt Bullard, Antonio Davis. I'm a business man, so I understand the economics of it all with football and money. But from an emotional standpoint, it hurt because what Dave Gavitt put together was so special."

ROGER MCCREADY, BOSTON COLLEGE: "I went from a state of disbelief, to being crushed, to being angry. I didn't think anyone could destroy something so special. The friendships, the camaraderie, the wars—to flush all that for the ACC, it angered me. The ACC? Really? We couldn't stand the ACC. We thought they were soft, and it's probably still that way. We used to love playing ACC teams, because we'd run over their chest, and smack them in the face."

JERRY MCCULLOUGH, PITTSBURGH: "The conference got too big. That's when the trouble started. Back in the day, if you went to UConn and upset them, you knew they were coming to your house hungry. Teams stopped playing each other twice."

LAWRENCE MOTEN, SYRACUSE: "It wasn't a good feeling at first. It made you realize that sports are all about economics. The traditions and the rivalries are gone. But times change, and I have enough experience to know that sometimes change can be a good thing. So I'm gonna take the good with the bad, and try to focus on the positives."

SHAWNELLE SCOTT, ST. JOHN'S: "Things started to change even back when Miami joined the conference. Don't get me wrong; we all loved going down there. But when you start adding all these football schools, things begin to filter out. When you have something that rich and you tamper with it, you lose something. It's not the same ethos. When Syracuse left, it was over. Kids don't rush to Big East schools anymore."

JERRY WALKER, SETON HALL: "[Seton Hall athletic director] Richie Regan was one of my mentors, and even back then, he said that football would be the death of the Big East. Being an alum of a school that's still in the conference, I'm not gonna sit here and say that it's the same. It's not. Not even close."

JOHN WALLACE, SYRACUSE: "It sucks. There's really no other way to put it. They should no longer be able to use the Big East name. Nothing against Butler, but who the fuck is Butler? I couldn't imagine having to travel to those places."

COLLEGE BASKETBALL GENERATES MASSIVE AMOUNTS OF MONEY, IN THE BILLIONS, AND THOSE CALLING FOR PLAYERS TO GET PAID ARE NO LONGER BEING IGNORED. AS A FORMER PLAYER, WHAT IS YOUR STANCE ON THE ISSUE?

BRYAN CAVER, SETON HALL: "I understand the premise behind it, but paying players would destroy the game. I know a lot of us came from impoverished backgrounds, but there'd be no way to regulate the system. Would I have loved to get paid? Absolutely. But if you do, it's no longer amateur athletics. It would detract from the college experience. Paying players would change the relationships between teammates, and all these years later, that's what I cherish the most: The time we spent off the court."

TERRY DEHERE, SETON HALL: "I think we have to come up with some sort of system of compensation for college players, since the best ones are so quick to leave. Nowadays, if you're a Top 10, Top 15 pick, you're entering the draft, even if you're not ready. The college game and the NBA suffer because of it. Right now, the rush to the NBA is greater than ever. No one has the patience or willingness to develop. If you compensate these guys, they'll stay in college and improve."

BOBBY MARTIN, PITTSBURGH: "Of course, they should get paid. The question is where do you draw the line. College basketball is a business, and the NCAA does people a disservice by acting like it's not. I didn't go to college to get an education. I went to get a job. We're not regular students, because we have more responsibility than the average kid. The NCAA uses players under the pretense that we're getting a free education. For what? For a job market that doesn't exist? Stop the bullshit. The NCAA has created this model where everyone is a winner, except the players. That has to change."

DWAYNE MCCLAIN, VILLANOVA: "I do think there should be a stipend. When you see the hundreds of millions of dollars these kids generate for their universities, why not share the wealth? They're no longer amateurs anyway. Yeah, their education is paid for, but it's a small pittance compared to what they're bringing in."

DARELLE PORTER, PITTSBURGH: "I think they should be given some money, but there has to be a cap to it. Otherwise, players will go to the highest bidder, and then you no longer have college sports. But I've been there, when all you have is your meal money, and instead of buying a healthy meal, you buy some cheap junk just to pocket a few bucks. Just because you get a scholarship to college doesn't mean that you all of a sudden have the money to eat or do anything else. I heard stories about how some players' families used to have to save for four years, just so they could have the money to travel to see their sons play for the first time on Senior Night. That isn't right."

ROBERT WERDANN, ST. JOHN'S: "I go back and forth on the issue, depending on the day. Players do so much for the university, and it reaps the rewards of their hard work. However, players do get paid. They're getting a free education. Whether they choose to take advantage of it, that's on them. Could schools put something aside for players for after they graduate? Maybe. But paying players on a weekly or monthly basis? I don't think so."

DOUG WEST, VILLANOVA: "I believe there should be some sort of compensation. Not many people understand the time that's committed to playing the sport. You have practice, film sessions, individual workouts, and training table, all in one day. Then, you're supposed to study? One thing I do know, having been a part of it, is that your value as a player far outweighs the value of a scholarship. Right now, I'm a Division III coach, and I'm going to have practice at noon. A few of my players won't be there because they'll have class. Life on the Division I level is nothing like that."

HYPOTHETICALLY SPEAKING, YOU GET TO PLAY THE ROLE OF COACH. YOUR TEAM IS TRAILING BY ONE POINT AND HAS THE BALL WITH 10 SECONDS REMAINING. IF YOU COULD CHOOSE ANY PLAYER IN BIG EAST HISTORY TO GIVE THE BALL TO, OTHER THAN YOURSELF, WHO WOULD IT BE?

RAFAEL ADDISON, SYRACUSE: "Pearl Washington. I wouldn't give the ball to anyone but him. He lived for the moment when the game was on the line. He could care less about what happened in the previous 39 minutes. He just wanted possession with a chance to win."

DONNY BROWN, PROVIDENCE: "I'm dumping it down low to O.T. [teammate Otis Thorpe]. He was built like a refrigerator, and could muscle the ball in through traffic. He was so raw back then, but you could see the talent was there. Look at his longevity in the NBA."

JOEY BROWN, GEORGETOWN: "I've got to keep it in the family, and pick [Georgetown's] Charles Smith. He was crafty and could always get his shot off."

BRYAN CAVER, SETON HALL: "Terry Dehere. He absolutely mastered our system. Dude could just fill it up. We all had our roles, and he didn't have many ball-handling responsibilities, so he could concentrate on scoring. The NBA tried to make him a point guard, but that wasn't his position."

OTIS HILL, SYRACUSE: "Billy Owens. Hands down. He was the original point-forward. When I got to Syracuse, I tried to mirror my game after his by handling the ball and shooting jumpers. Coach Boeheim was like, 'Uh, no, get in the post.'"

MALCOLM HUCKABY, BOSTON COLLEGE: "Allen Iverson. I was in the Sixers' rookie camp the same time as him, and they had us play one-on-one to like six or seven. When he had game-point, he elevated for the shot, and yelled 'Game' before the ball even left his hand. And believe it or not, I'd take [teammate] Gerrod Abram a close second. He had three buzzer-beaters in one season."

JAREN JACKSON, GEORGETOWN: "Alonzo Mourning. When I was a senior, he was a freshman. He came in like a veteran, and had a cockiness about him. He had

89

so much confidence, and demanded the ball at critical times in the game. Right away, I felt comfortable giving it to him, and he produced. The way he and Dikembe went at it in practice, as a guard, you just couldn't get a shot off. They'd compete against each other to see who could lead the team in blocks. That's when I figured I just better take my jump shots, and be happy with it. The hell with going to the basket."

KERRY KITTLES, VILLANOVA: "Chris Mullin was money. He was like a left-handed Larry Bird. I played against him in the NBA when he was a lot older, when he wasn't *the* Chris Mullin, but my goodness! You hear people talk about what this player would be like if he had that player's athleticism, or what that player would be like if he had this player's shooting ability. If Chris Mullin was just a little bit faster, oh, man! He was just that good."

JASON LAWSON, VILLANOVA: "Kerry Kittles. He'll either make the shot, or make the play that leads to the shot. He kept going and going. I never saw him tired at the end of a game. And he had the right temperament for that situation. Kerry never got too up or too down."

BOBBY MARTIN, PITTSBURGH: "Dana Barros. He could shoot from 50 feet. He was in range all the time. I was just happy I never had to guard him. If he had the ball, it was over."

DWAYNE MCCLAIN, VILLANOVA: "Pearl Washington. With the things he could do with the ball, you have to give it to him and let him create."

ROGER MCCREADY, BOSTON COLLEGE: "Definitely Pearl. He wasn't the best jump-shooter, but he could get in the lane whenever he wanted, and there was nothing you could do about it. I'll never forget my sophomore year, playing them in the dome. At the end of the game, one of my teammates [Martin Clark] hit a layup and got fouled. The score was tied with four seconds left, and the free throw would've won the game. But he missed. Pearl got the ball, weaved through traffic, and let one fly from half-court that just beat the buzzer. But he never stopped running. By the time the ball went through the net, he was close to the tunnel, because he never broke stride. The fans stormed the court, and he was in the locker room. To this day, I'd never seen anything like that. I've seen plenty of buzzer-beaters, but the guy is still standing on the court when it goes through."

DARELLE PORTER, PITTSBURGH: "Either Jason Matthews or Sean Miller. Both of them could draw a foul and were automatic from the line."

DAVID RUSSELL, ST. JOHN'S: "Chris Mullin. No question about it. I remember our first workout with him. When I saw his big, puffy hair and his short shorts, I said, 'There's no way in hell this guy can play ball. I'm guarding him.' That was it—he nailed like eight straight shots on me. You couldn't drop your hands for a second. His release was that quick. You couldn't let him breathe. Any inch you gave him, it was over. Coach said, 'I told you that son of a bitch can play.'"

RONY SEIKALY, SYRACUSE: "Chris Mullin. It doesn't matter where the shot was, or the situation that he was in. He would have already practiced it 1,000 times. He was the ultimate gym rat. His athletic level was mediocre, but his work ethic and his skill was off the charts. And to me, that made him even greater than he was. I'd die with him at the end of a game in a heartbeat."

DOUG WEST, VILLANOVA: "I want Mark Jackson penetrating and kicking it out to Chris Mullin."

Acknowledgments

THIS BOOK WOULD NOT HAVE BEEN POSSIBLE without the input of all the former players who were interviewed, so they need to be thanked first. Not only do I appreciate the time each of you spent talking with me and sharing your stories, I also cherish the memories I have of watching you compete. As a basketball fan who grew up in suburban Philadelphia in the post-Big Five era, the Big East Conference meant everything to me.

I love the sport. Always have and always will. No matter how old I get, I'll never stop feeling the childlike excitement I feel upon seeing a tournament bracket for the first time. Whether it's the NCAAs, the NIT, or the scores of conference tourneys, I'm like a meteorologist with his weather map when the calendar turns to March. I weigh each condition in trying to plot out every scenario imaginable. And I track underdogs like Al Roker does low-pressure systems.

Thank you to Dennis Nappi II, my publisher who took a chance on a project outside of his box. I also want to give a shout-out to the Sports Information Directors at each school—especially Syracuse's Pete Moore, Connecticut's Phil Chardis, Pittsburgh's Matt Plizga, Seton Hall's Thomas Chen, Boston College's Matt Lynch, Mekale Jackson at St. John's, Miami's Amy Woodruff LaBrie, and Georgetown's Mex Carey—who provided photos and thus helped to illustrate the book. No sportswriter can reach his or her full potential without the images that bring words to life.

I want to express my gratitude for my family, my parents Jim and Kathy and brother Matt and sister Beth. Your support has sustained me at each step of my journey. And all the love in the world belongs with my wife Allison and sons Holden and Sebastian. You three are the light of my life, and give me more than I could ever give back in return.

Lastly, thank you to the written word. It seems that every time I have searched for something in my life, regardless of what it is, I end up finding it in you.

Service of Change, LLC

"Small changes among the masses can have a massive impact around the world."

Be The Change!

www.ServiceOfChange.com

CPSIA information can be obtained
at www.ICGtesting.com
Printed in the USA
BVHW040806250420
578457BV00014B/3061

9 780692 669136